LORD,
I AM DEPENDING
ON YOU

Written by MaryJane Edwards

Printed in the United States of America

ISBN-10: 1540775801
ISBN-13: 978-1540775801

10 9 8 7 6 5 4 3 2

Empire Publishing
www.empirebookpublishing.com

Have you ever been in a situation where things start to go wrong all around you?

Have you ever been lonely and sad? Have you ever felt like no matter how hard you tried to do good, that things would just get worse and worse in your life? Have you ever felt like just giving up!? Well this book has all the answer to those questions and more. God has a son name Jesus has promised to never leave you thru all your trials and tribulations, your good and bad times. Jesus has always been there right beside you. He says that you have not because you ask not. Learn how to call upon the name of Jesus and how to go to him in prayer for help with all of your problems. Learn how to stop putting him last and how to put him FIRST in your life!

He loves you. He really does. Show him how much you love him!

The book is to inform young people of how God say we are to love him and others. My aim is to reach out to every young person and any one that do not know the Lord to guide them toward God and his son Jesus with this book. There are 375 titled pages in this manuscript filled with scriptures from the Bible with messages that will encourage, inspire and strengthen anyone that dare to read it!

The book tells how to love your enemies, to put others first, to be a servant for God, to have a mind of your own, to love your parents, school and not cherish material things. How to not be a bully, but to help the poor and needy, to not be afraid to go to school and so much more encouraging words on how to survive in this world with God by your side. Once you start to read, it is very hard to stop.

I want to reach out to the elementary, middle, and high schools, colleges, group homes, detention centers, churches and the world to make sure that every young person and old hear about this book! This book is designed to save a soul because it has God and his son Jesus in it!

Dedication

Praise Ye the Lord! I acknowledge him, dedicate this book to him and thank him for blessing me with the desire to write this inspiring book. I could not have completed this book without him. I pray that this encouraging book change each and every heart around the world, to love and be a servant for the Lord. The Holy Spirit inspired me to write this book to reach out to every young boy and girl, teenagers and anyone that do not know the Lord. The message will brighten anyone that is going thru some hard times that need to find their way! A book that will lift their spirit about the love of God and Jesus and how he love everyone. It do not make a difference what is going on in anyone's life, he will always help and be there for the world. The book is written in a form that is easy for anyone to comprehend when you use your Bible or study Bible. This is an inspirational, devotional, guidance book with scriptures from the Bible.

Every page will draw you closer and closer to God. Everyone needs to know about God and his son Jesus and how to love one another. This book will definitely show you how to love and grow closer to the Lord. May this book be a blessing to my husband, George Edwards, Jr. To my children, Hope Darnika Sims, Larry Pernelle Sims, Tiffani Camille Rudolph, Lance Jermelle Sims and my Grandchildren; Dyshon Dominigue Fuller, Christine Marie Long, Michaela Marie Long, Lance Jermelle Sims, Jr. Emori Inez Sims, Landyn Derrell Sims, Avery Marshall Sims, Chance Javari Sims, Larry Pernelle Sims, Jr. Jada Nikeya Sims, Alissia Diamond Sims, Josiah Kyree Sims, Dontayan

Tariq Sims, Leilani Camille Rudolph, Justin Demon Rudolph, Jr., Justice Kaneal Rudolph and my cousin Janice Pitzer who kept encouraging me to never give up. Also to my mother, Mary Alice Edward sand all of my sisters and their family and the entire world!

"But seek ye first the kingdom of God, and his righteousness; and all these things shall be added unto you. " Matthew 6:33 (KJV)

LORD, I AM DEPENDING ON YOU

Introduction

This inspirational book is written in a form to touch the young, old and the teenager's heart and mind in a way to help them understand. I want to make it easy for them to see the picture and how to love and thank Jesus and to connect with him on a daily basis. This is a book to be read every day to keep their mind focus on God and life. The Holy Spirit put it upon my heart to write this devotional guide for every teenager that love the Lord and for the one that cannot find their way. I was a teenager that loves the Lord but I grew up sad because I could not find my way.

I went to Sunday school, church, Bible study, and prayer meetings on Wednesday night and choir rehearsal on Thursday evening with my family every week. I was still lost because I did not understand what was being taught to me because it became a routine that I followed because I knew this is what my parents wanted me and my sisters to do. My mind was not really there because there were things happening at my home that kept me unhappy and very afraid. I was terrified of my father when I was a teenager because he made it plain for us not to tell anyone anything that was going on in our home. So I did what was told and went along with pretending that I was happy; when all along I was counting the days until I reach the age of eighteen when I could finally leave home. So this going to church and being in church all the time is something me and my sisters had to go thru with church because that was how it was back then when I was growing up. My parents were content just to have us in church whether we were getting something out of it or not. Why I say this is because we were never questioned about what we had learned in church. I wish it could have been a devotional guidance book like this out for teenagers when I was a teenager. It would have saved me so much heartache and pain as I tried to find my way in this world when I was not totally committed to God. I had to find out things the hard way. I missed out on so much from going my own way instead of seeking the help of the Lord. I pray that each person that take the time to read this book will draw closer to the Lord and ask God for his guidance and that each message will strengthen them and change their life for the better to be a servant for the Lord. May God Bless you.

Table of Contents

A Merry Heart

Putting the best on the outside while trusting in the Lord is a healthy thing. Everyone has problems. No one's life is peaches and cream. God Holy words are powerful. They give you life, something to lean on knowing that you do not have to worry if you put your faith in him. Do not concentrate on the problem; concentrate on what God say he will do if you let him into your life.

Be happy with happy thoughts, with your mind on Jesus and all he has done for you. Just knowing that Jesus love you should keep you happy with a happy spirit to share with the world.

Proverbs 15:13, 15
Psalm 119:35
Psalm 25:4

If You Are a Thief

It is always best to work for what you want in life. Do not try to think of a fast way to make money.

This will (the majority of the time) cause problems that will get you in trouble. When you work hard for something, it will make you appreciate it more in the long run. If you have a desire to take and pick up things that are not yours, pray, then ask God to take that desire out of your heart. Ask for forgiveness. He can heal you and restore you from any sickness. Make an honest living!

Ephesians 4:28
Isaiah 55:7
Psalm 62:10

Let Your Words be an Encouragement

When telling your peers about the Lord, never be discouraged with unbelievers when they abuse you. Be courteous and respectful to everyone that you meet. Being humble can be hard when the enemy is right beside you with harsh words. Sometimes when you are around your peers you might have some that might curse and be rude to you. Instead of coming down to their level with them, show your peers how easy it is to be kind and loving in the way that you talk to people. Let your conversation be from a good heart. You are showing in a beautiful way how to tell people about the Lord. How to serve the Lord and to be kind to others!

Colossians 4:6
Ephesians 4:29

Lambs among Wolves

Every day of your life you are going to go thru the good and the bad. God did not create anyone special on this earth to not go thru some trying hard times. When you become a Christian, Satan will try to attack you in almost everything that you do. Throw fear aside and let God and his Holy words fight for you. The more you are attacked, the more closer you get to the Lord. It may feel sometimes like the enemy is all around you. Do not panic! God's Holy words will clear the way for you and keep Satan back. God will always have his Holy angels all around you. So do not fear!

The more you serve the Lord and live for him, the more the enemy will come around you to make it hard for you. But always trust in the Lord and stand by and watch the salvation of the Lord!

Never stop spreading the good news about Jesus!

Luke 10:3
Matthew 10:16

4

A Ram in the Bush

Just when you thought there was no hope, when you really needed help with a situation, someone always came thru for you. God is the one that sent that blessing your way. What is so good about God is that He will step in and help you even when you are not living right - When your friends and family has turn their back on you. God is the one that will have mercy on you and help you when everyone else has thrown you away. Know that when all else has failed you, look to the Lord. He is the ram in the bush. He will always provide and be there for you.

Philippians 4:19
Psalm 40:1
Psalm 27:14

Be Happy with Yourself

So things are not going the way that you planned. It is very easy to tell someone what you think you want out of life. But it is another thing when your plans go the opposite way. Do not give up on yourself. I do not know if anyone told you or not but when you include God in everything that you do. He is the one that make great things happen. You have to want to seek him. Want to know him. Want to love him. Want to serve him. Reach out to God in prayer. Do not ever think that you are a failure because you are not! God love you! Be happy knowing that he created you. He has good things for you to do for him that will enrich your life and the life of others. So be happy! Be happy! Be happy!

James 5:13
Psalm 103:1-2

6

God is the Rock

If you have God in your life, you have something to jump for joy about. We are blessed to have a God that is eternal that will be with us forever. Why do people when bad things happen turn to anyone but the Lord? They always wait until they have run out of options then they will go to the Lord. Do you know that he has never left you! He said that he would never leave you or forsake you and that is the truth! Put your faith and trust in him. Find ways to serve him. Tell people about him and to always worship and praise him. He is the one that love you. Will never hurt you and will stand by you thru your trials and tribulations. Give him your best! Do your best! After all, he is the best!

Deuteronomy 32:4
Genesis 49:24

True Serenity

Your life has no time for fear and worriation. Worrying will not make problems go away. Show God how much you love and trust him! Choose peace knowing that any trouble that may occur is only temporary when you put your faith in God who is the ruler over the universe. God is in control of the future. There is no need to worry because you cannot change life. The Bible will be fulfilled. God is not a liar! So be happy and content as you work toward getting closer to the Lord. Know that peace is the presence of God which bring serenity and a peace of mind.

Roman 5:1
1John 5:4-5

Rejoice in the Lord

I have been thru so much in my life. God has come thru for me in so many awful circumstances. The heartaches that I experience made me a stronger person where it strengthens my faith in God. It made me realize that I could do nothing without God. I know how it feels to be hurt and wanting. I know how it feels to be blessed and not wanting. It changed my heart to when things would go wrong, like when my lights and my water would get cut off, the car break down, or to have to tell my children that they would not be getting anything for Christmas. I would still go to work with a smile on my face knowing, trusting and believing that God would make a way for me. People would walk up to me and say you have been thru so much and you continue to smile.

It made me feel good to smile and be happy, even though I had problems. I was happy because the Lord was with me and he was in control. I knew that he would fix everything for me and he did! Get close to the Lord. Love him with all of your heart and keep him first in your life!

I Thessalonica 2: 19-20
Romans 8:28
Philippians 4:4
Psálm 126: 5-6

If someone hurt your feelings - do not take it personally

If you ever run into someone with an attitude problem that cut you down with harsh words.

Something could be troubling the person with a lot of things going wrong in their life. They are taking it out by talking that way to the first person that come along. Do not let it get to you! Just be quiet and listen. Pray for them! It takes two people to argue. When you do not say anything, they will look at you and it usually will die down. Then later that same person who hurt your feelings will have time to think about what they did and will come back to say that they are sorry. Think about what would Jesus do in a situation like this and you will always get it right!

Keep peace!

I Peter 3: 10-12
Psalm 34: 13
Hebrew 12:14

Be a worker in the Church

Be happy to work in God's church! There is so much work to do in the church. You can start by being a peace maker and not a gossiper. Yes gossipers are in the church. The church is a place for worship, not haters. If you or you know someone that come to church to stir up trouble. Pray and ask God to put love in their heart where there is hate. Show your love for everyone. Do not judge or say anything negative about anyone. We are to be imitators just like Jesus. The work that you do for the church is for the Lord. Enter the church with thanksgiving and praise. The churches need a lot of young people that are willing to dedicate their time to the Lord. So many young people think church is for older people. It is for everyone. God needs workers in the church such as Ushers, Choir members, Missionaries, Ministers, and Deacons, and Sunday school teachers. Do your very best for the Lord. He always gives us his best!

I Corinthians 14: 33, 40
I Timothy 3: 14-15

I'm Still Here

Think back on all what you have been thru in your life. No one in this world has had a perfect life. We all have been thru something. But thru it all, God was right there with you. He saw and heard everything with his grace and his mercy. He was there! He was the one that made things right when they were going wrong. He was the one that turn that no into a yes. He was the one that brought peace in your life when so much burden was on you. God is always with you protecting you from this sinful world. Thank him for loving you even when you were ready to give up on yourself. Thank him for shielding you from the enemy and for his Holy words the Bible that is so powerful. He kept you and never left you. He is the reason you are still here!

Psalm 50:14-15
Psalm 86:13

Abstinence

Learn to respect God by taking care of your body. Being a teenager, hanging with your peers that have different belief about life, and God take a strong minded person to resist the temptations of sin. God want you to be obedient to his Holy words and have respect for your body. How can you miss something that you have never had? Saying no to a young man that want to have sex is not embarrassing! It is the right thing to do. This is a big responsibility for the young lady and the young man. A young man if he really care for the young lady he would never ask her for sex. Can you imagine all the things that could happen?! She could catch a disease, get pregnant and that could involve so many people - Your parents, money for medication and a child. Some young People think that when they mess up they can just get a prescription for the disease, have an abortion or give the child up for adoption. But think about it! If it is a sexual transmitted disease, your body could easily be changed especially if it is Syphilis or Gonorrhea. Now if the young lady get pregnant, that is another life that you have to think about. No unborn child should be aborted or given up for adoption. It might seem like something easy to take care of but it is not. Whichever option you make, it is a sin. God see everything that you do and whatever you do in the dark it will come back to haunt you later.

Take time to think about what you do and do not let a friend or your peer's talk you into doing something that you will regret later on in your life. God want you to have fun growing up as a teenager; not bring sexual immorality sin against your body. He wants you to live right and to care about your body in a very respectful way. *"Flee fornication. Every sin that a man doeth is without the body; but he that committeth fornication sinneth against his own body."* **I Corinthians 6:18 KJV**

Just say no!

II Timothy 2:22
I Timothy 6:11

I am a Winner

You cannot help but progress when you have the Lord on your side. You can wake up every morning, full of energy. Excited about your day because you know that you have the Lord working on your behalf, to show you the way and guide your every step. You trust him with your life. To feel secured in everything that you do is a healthy and peaceful sensation for your body.

You cannot help but be a winner when you have the love of God in your heart. Enjoy life, serve the Lord, tell everyone about him so that they can become winners also.

Psalm 25:8
Psalm 32:8
Psalm 34:15

Wonderful Blessings

Thank you God for protecting me at home, at school, on my job, on the highway, on the school bus. at the mall, at the baseball, basketball and football games. At the skating rink, the movies, at church, on vacation and even at the grocery store! At the doctor office, at the amusement park, at the pool. We are to thank God for so many blessings because he is the one that watches over us and who have his Holy angels all around us. We are to never take him for granted. Praise him and thank him every day of your life. He is so worthy to be praise.

John 1:16
Proverbs 13:21
Psalm 108:1

Do not skip School

Teachers that are agitated, short patience, and rude with no care attitudes is enough to make any student skip school. Plus trouble that come along with students that have problems of their own that bring it to school with them! Skipping school is the easy way out. It is so easy to just give up! Do not let people unhealthy ways turn you around. Hold your head up, stand boldly, and move forward with God on your side. Always know that he is always with you protecting you. Just call on him and he will come to show you the way with love. He will lighten your load, put joy in your heart where you will feel as if you can conquer anything or anybody. So do not miss classes or avoid school! Make it your business to attend school with God right beside you! He stays ready!

I Peter 1:7
Isaiah 48:11

Have a Mind of your Own

Being around so many teens and young people you will see and hear all kind of things that will be tempting to you. The line that a lot of teens love to use is; I bet you are afraid to try this! A lot of teens do not want to be embarrassed in front of another teen but it is always best to do what is right than what is wrong. Have a strong mind of your own, and then no one can talk you into trouble that could ruin your life later. Think of Jesus! Focus on how he would handle the situation. Do not do wrong trying to please your peers.

Matthew 6:13
I John 5:18-19

Eternity

Our life here on earth is not permanent. We are here for just a little while. We are here for a purpose. We are to ask the Lord what is it that he has for us to do for him. God have work for us to do. It is a good thing to know that we are going to leave this world one day and go to live with him in heaven. But while we are here we are to love God with all our heart and soul. We are to love one another. Help the poor and needy and widowers. Tell everyone how Jesus died on the cross for all of our sins so that we may live. Do not waste your time doing nothing for the Lord.

Make the best of your time and do all that you can for the Lord. He is all that we need.

Psalm 39:5-6
I Peter 1:24

Drunkeness

The Holy Spirit lives in us when we become Christians. It keeps us humble on how to live right.

Our bodies are not our own. It belongs to God and we are to keep it healthy. Who told you it was fun to hang out with your friends and get loaded!? You are fooling yourself if you think this is cool because it is not! This is a picture of where teens try to impress one another by showing that they are not afraid to try something dangerous and that they have it going on because they have a bottle of alcohol. Drinking alcohol is something that can become addictive and will eventually destroy you! The problem that you had before you took the drink will still be there after you become sober! Satan is out to wreck your life. He wants to see you destroy yourself and others! You know, you can show that you have it going on when you do not participate in this deadly routine of drinking alcohol. Take time to find Jesus. Whatever you are going thru, tell Jesus about it. The high that you get from alcohol is temporary. The peace of mind and love that Jesus give is everlasting!

I Corinthian 6: 19-20
Ephesians 5:18-19
Proverbs 23: 29-35

Do not go around thinking you are better than anyone

Who told you that you fell from heaven and was all that! No one is better than the other person.

We all can get sick, die and leave here at any time! If you do not know how to appreciate someone, ask God to show you. Do not be so quick to toot your nose up at people without getting to know them. The very person you stick your nose up at will probably be the main person that will help you when no one else will and become your friend! To show kindness and love can be hard if you make it hard. Take time to get to know Jesus. He can show you how to get rid of all that selfishness and hate. Let him be your guide. He will lead you to love and show you how to use it!

Proverb 16: 18-19
Psalm 101:5

How deep is your Love?

The timid, the humble, the meek and mild. You actually have teens with loving spirits like these that are in your school. The majority of them are the ones that are bullied in school. When you come upon a student that has these characteristics, show your love. Let them know that they are appreciated. These are the students that are obedient to their parents, respectful to others, come to school to learn. Do not hate on them! Try to learn something from them. They could become the best friend you ever had! Show love.

I Corinthians 13:4-5
I Corinthians 10:24

Get to know God!

Some people might ask, how do I get to know God? You can start by reading the Bible, his Holy words. Find a church to attend, go to Bible study. You can learn so much about the Lord. Pray to him, ask him for guidance. Take time to spend some quiet time in an area where you can sit and talk to the Lord. That time is for you and the Lord. It is a comforting experience to feel peace and love as you diligently seek the Lord. You will find that being with the Lord feel so good. You can talk to him and tell him how much you love him and thank him for all that he has done for you. Send your praises up to him daily. Seek a close relationship with God as you get to know him. Read the Bible more and more each day as you pray to God for understanding. He is worth getting to know!

Psalm 143:8
Genesis 28:10-15
Exodus 33:11
Nehemiah 10:28

Do not worry about everyday Life

God told us that he would supply all of our needs and he meant it! That mean do not put your trust in man but in God! He will provide the food that you need and anything else that come up!

He is the one that put money in your pocket, provide you with clothing and a roof over your head. Do not depend on your job! Put all your trust in God because he is the one that made it possible for you to get that job. God always make a way out of no way for anyone that has faith in him.

Luke 12: 22-24
Job 38:41

UnGodly People

Do not ignore the truth about God to live the kind of lifestyle you prefer. God's Holy Bible speak the truth! It talk about sinful people in the old and new testament. The sinful things that people were doing back then they are doing them now. Get on board with the Lord and live for him before it is too late! Make a change in your life to seek God and to serve him and live for him. Make a change for a peace of mind and to live forever with the Lord! Glory to his name!

Romans 8:9
II Corinthians 5:17
Isaiah 65:17
Galatians 6:15

Material Things

In our everyday life we are to be satisfied with what we have. Do no envy people that are rich or your peers that have everything they could ever wish for. Those THINGS cannot make you happy. Those THINGS are temporary happiness that will bring you sadness. God is all the happiness we will ever need and want in this life and the next. He is the love that will forever be with you when you live for him and not worship THINGS and MONEY. Keep your mind on God, not THINGS!

Proverbs 15:27
Proverbs 23: 4-5
Proverbs 28: 20
I Timothy 6:9

Look to God for Guidance and Leadership

The Lord will protect you as you trust and put your faith in him. He is the one that instruct you and teach you the way you should go in life when you put your life in his hands. At all times, acknowledge him and know that it is he who bless you and that help you along your journey. He will never leave you. Even when you want to give up on yourself he will be there. Always be willing to follow his directions!

John 10: 3-5
Isaiah 30:21
Isaiah 58:11

Winning a Race

Being a Christian is not an easy task! You will be tested and tempted by Satan. Always finish what you set out to do for the Lord. Use the inner strength and staying power that you were bless with to work for the Lord. There will be hardship and obstacles that will try to stop or slow you down. But you stay strong and geared up with God's Holy words, with prayer, with Bible study and with God continually in your life! As Christians we are trying to make it to heaven.

Diligently seek the Lord. Prepare yourself to step out and tell others about Jesus. Reach out to the homeless, the poor, the drunk, drug addict and prostitutes. To anyone that do not have God in their life. Working for the Lord is worth every second you put in it.

I Corinthians 9:25-26
I Timothy 6:12

God love reaches every corner of the World

As you work toward having a close relationship with the Lord, your Faith will get stronger as you trust in him. You will see and feel God's surrounding love that reaches more than you could ever imagine. His love covers what each of us go thru in all our trials. It reaches out to everyone and everything. No matter what affliction you go thru; God's love for us is anchored. Nothing will ever be able to keep us apart from the presence of Jesus. God's love is forever. He is not going anywhere!

Ephesians 3:18-19
Psalm 107:43

Be Kind to your Dog

One of the worst things you can do to an animal is to mistreat it. They have feeling; they need love, affection and attention. When you take up time with them, they will show their love and appreciation. Do not shut them up in a small pen where they cannot walk around and get exercise where they just lay down the majority of the day. What good is they for to be penned in a small cage and you feed and give them water when you get ready?! What kind of life do they have when they are sleeping in an area where they urinate and have a bowel movement also! Would you want to be kept like that?! The same way an evil spirit can get in a human, it can get in an animal where it might turn against you! Pray over your dog and thank the Lord for your dog. If you do not have time for the dog, give it to someone that do have time. Remember God see everything that you do and you have to give account of everything that you do here on this earth.

Proverb 12:10
Psalm 147:9
Genesis 1:28

I Will Survive

You may live in a home where the mother and father fight all the time. Your parents may be alcoholics. They may go out to night clubs and party all the time. You may come home from school and the house is a wreck. There is no food to eat and everywhere you look you do not see anything but sadness all around you. Do not sit there and feel as if you have nowhere to go or anyone to talk to. Go to the Lord in prayer and tell him that you need him. Do not feel ridiculous or like you are doing something crazy. God will answer your prayer. He will help you and show you how to bring restoration in your home. He wants you to put all your faith and trust in him. He did not tell you to fix it! You have survived because he has always been with you. With God you will always survive!

I Thessalonians 5:17
Romans 8:26-27

We All Have Sinned

Do not look down on people who have sinned and are sinning. Everyone has sinned except Jesus Christ. He is the only one that is perfect! Whatever sin you have committed, repent of your sins and God will forgive you if you ask him. Do not think less of yourself for sinning. God is here for everyone, not just for the people that are living right. Do not ever be ashamed to ask God to forgive you. He love you. He will not turn his back on you. People have lied, committed adultery, had abortions, stole, killed, beat up on people, child molester, been a stripper, and did so many other things and God forgave them. He is not like people that will throw stuff back up in your face later. Once he forgives you, he forgives you. Case close!

Romans 3:23
Hebrew 9:12

Never Support anyone that is plotting to do wrong!

Friends can be a tough word sometimes because everyone is not your friend! Some young people want to fit in at school or colleges because they meet people they call their friends that become important to many of them. Their friend becomes someone they can talk to and share everything with. I say to be a true friend, always be honest to them whether they like it or not. If you ever see a change in your friend and you see that they are going down or backward, instead of going forward in life, talk to see what is going on. If the person has change to where they are talking about doing something weird or evil to themselves or others, try to talk to them and steer them in the right direction to the Lord, then pray for them. Tell them about Jesus and go to the concordance in the back of your Bible to read scriptures on whatever the problem is. True friends help each other. Not go down the wrong road together! Show that you care by speaking up!

Proverb 13:20
Proverb 2:20

God the Author

The Bible was inspired by God. No one is to change the word of God. The person that does this awful thing will have to answer to God at judgment day. There are many people that will change the word of God and think nothing of it. When you quote and direct people wrong with what the word of God really mean, you are representing a picture of something that is false. Whenever someone quotes something from the Bible, always ask where can it be found in the Bible? Ask what chapter and verse! God breathe it, inspired it, conceived it and authenticated it! Do not ever change the word of God. Meditate on it! Love it and live it!

Galatians 1: 11-12
II Peter 1:20-21
Proverbs 30:6

Stealing

Have your friends ever asked you to go shopping at the mall with them just when you did not have any money? I loved to go with my friends to the mall but not without any money. They would beg me to go but I would never go because I knew I would see something I wanted just when I did not have any money. A lot of times this is how some people get in trouble. They see something that they really want that become tempting to where they will steal it! Do not be tempted at going to places and doing something that could ruin your life! When I was in my teens, my older sister and I use to love to go skating on Thursday night. My father made it plain that if we did not save our allowance money he would not give us more money just to go skating. So a friend suggested that we steal a pair of stockings out the store, and then take the stockings back to get the money. Back in my day you did not need a receipt to get your refund. Well, it worked with me but my sister got caught stealing! They were going to call the police on her but I walked up to the manager and told her that she was sorry and that we would never come back in their store. They told us to get out of their store! That was the scariest feeling and all for trying to get money just to go skating! We both could have gone to jail! Stealing is carrying a burden. We never tried that again. God want us to be honest, trustworthy and not to steal anything. Working for what you want feels a whole lot better than STEALING!

Leviticus 19:11
Exodus 20:15

Trouble

When trouble comes your way, stand strong on God's Holy words. He will do what he says he will do. Trial and tribulations are inescapable for people that are close to the Lord. Jesus said that the believers would be persecuted for my sake. As you go thru life telling people about Jesus, people are going to be mean and cruel to you. But rejoice and know that the Lord is with you.

I Thessalonians 3:3
II Timothy 3:12
Acts 14:22

Introduction to Eternity

Look at this life as an introduction to eternal life with God. You are only visiting here on earth. This is not our permanent home. When you leave this earth, your eternal life will have no more sickness, death, sin, or evil. This is an awesome thing to look forward to and that is to live forever with the Lord. We are not to get so comfortable with this world and the material things in it. Which is temporary, but to seek the Lord and be a servant for him which is eternal. Live so God can use you in this world and the next!

Ecclesiastes 3:11
Ecclesiastes 8:17
Isaiah 55:8

Be Joyful Now!

Do not think that being a Christian mean living a dull life. There is so much joy in being around true Christians that love the Lord. So many people shy away and will not come to the Lord from hearing so many negative things from people that do not come to church. Those types of people do not want to come to the house of the Lord and they try hard to stop anyone else from coming to the Lord. Do not miss out on your blessing of knowing and loving the Lord that is greater than happiness. Seek God's direction and guidance for living. The Lord wants you to enjoy life. The beautiful privacy to joy is God's visibility inside of you. With God, joy is forever lasting. Learn how you can find satisfaction in his presence. Rejoice in the Lord!

Proverb 16:20
Ecclesiastes 3:12-13
Ecclesiastes 2:24

Come as you are

Do not sit around making up crazy excuses telling the Lord that you will get SAVED when you learn how to love your mother or your father more or when you get your life right. That you are ashamed of all the sin you have committed! That you need to have nice clothes to go to church or you are waiting to get that nice home so you will feel comfortable inviting people over for Bible study. If you are waiting for things to be perfect to give your life to the Lord, then hear this! You have a long wait! Do not find excuses that can hold you back from loving and serving the Lord.

If you love the Lord, nothing in this world can stop you from spreading the good news about him! Go to Jesus on your bended knees and ask him to forgive you for your sins. Start your journey for the Lord now! Jesus is not looking for people with a perfect figure, nice car or someone that is very educated. He want you just as you are, NOW! If you are broke with no money, sick, homeless, a drunk, a liar, a thief, a drug addict, or whatever you may be, he want you! He really do! Pray, ask the Lord what is it that he want you to do for him? Then reach out to others to tell them about the Lord. Be a follower of Jesus today!

Luke 10:2-3
John 4:35
Matthew 9:37-38

The Love of Money

Money has fooled a lot of people so many times by having them to think that they would actually be so happy with a lot of money. How do you be happy with something that is only temporary? Everything that you buy with money is going to waste away. You come in this world without anything and you will surely leave without anything. You cannot take anything with you when you leave. God bless you with money to be more concerned with helping the poor and needy people and to look out for people that are struggling. God did not intend for people to stack up their riches and brag about all that they have. You are to love God and your fellowman more than money. When God bless you where you have a nice home to lay your head and a nice car, nice clothing's, plenty of food and a nice bank account, how can you live not trying to help someone in need. It is the best feeling in the world when you give to the needy. The high that you get when you BUY and SHOP is something that is temporary. Do not let the love of money stop you from blessing someone. Serve God and be a cheerful giver! Concentrate more on God than money! There is nothing in heaven you can buy with money!

Proverbs 23:4
Proverbs 28:20
Matthew 6:19
James 5:1-5
Matthew 6:24
Ecclesiastes 10:19

Prostitutes

God is a forgiving God. He will forgive even a prostitute of their sins. Ask for forgiveness and start a new life to live for the Lord. Take care of yourself and have respect for yourself. As you grow up and go thru life you will be tempted to do sinful things. Whether you are a male or female do not ever let anyone lead you to a life of destruction by destroying your body doing sinful things. Our bodies are to stay pure and to be used for God's glory.

Proverbs 7: 6-27
I Corinthians 6:15
I Thessalonians 4:3-4

The Eyes of the Lord

The Lord can see everything. So whatever you do that is wrong, he see it and know all about it. If you think you can fool God you are wasting your time. With man, you can pull pranks, tell lies, and get away sometime but never with God. Even though there are so many evil people in the world, killing all around us, God has his eyes on them and you! Do not give up on life or God! The harder life become, the stronger and more you lean on Jesus. Meditate on him and trust him.

He is not going anywhere!

Psalm 34:15-16
Proverbs 15:3
Hebrews 4:13
Job 34:21

His Eye is on the Sparrow

Do not think that when you step out in the world on your own that you are alone. God is always with you. Even though you cannot see him, he is there. You can walk with confidence knowing that he has his angels all around you. He keeps you safe from the enemy and he is always ready to fight your battle for you. So do not be afraid of the terrible things of this world or what horrible situations that tries to come upon you. God will always watch over you. Feel safe just knowing the Lord. He is the one that has promise to take care of you, not man! Lean on God with confidence knowing that he will NEVER fail!

II Samuel 22:31
Proverbs 30:5
Psalm 71: 1-5, 7,8
Psalm 61:3

You can keep God in School

It looks as if high authority in school and many other places are trying to keep God and his son Jesus out of school. But do not be dismayed. No one can stop you from praising him, talking to him, praying to him, representing him and loving him if you really love God! You can talk to God anytime and anywhere. If you are ever frighten for some reason at school and you fear your life is in danger call on the name of Jesus. There is power in his name. Remember your time with

God is between you and him! Always show your dedication and love for him. He will do the same for you!

Psalm 78:4-7
Psalm 22:30
Joshua 22:5

Get down on your knees

People worship the Lord in so many different ways. With a lift of their hands, with a song and a dance or with a loud or silent prayer on their knees. Kneeling in worship shows divine humility and devotion toward the Lord. When you welcome Jesus Christ into your life, show your love and dedication to him. Do not be a hypocrite by saying one thing and showing no interest in him around your peers. He sees everything that you do. Be proud to acknowledge the Lord. Let the world know that you love him and need him in all that you do. Adoration for him should always bring us to our knees. For Jesus Christ is Lord forever!

Psalm 95: 6-7
Matthew 15: 8-9
Romans 14:11

Choose the right Path

The majority of times when young people are brought up in a Christian home for some reason as they get older and move out into the world on their own. They decide to forget about their

Christian upbringing and become a person that cannot wait to go to wild parties, strip clubs, try drugs, curse, wear seductive clothing, date married men's and do so many other sinful things.

Some show this behavior with no shame, as if they have to do those things as if they had been missing something. Believe me, you are not missing anything! Do not be so fast to follow the sinful crowd by doing things that will ruin your life. Pray to the Lord. Ask him to guide your footsteps, to put you on the right path. You will always need the Lord to survive in this world.

Let him be your guide.

Proverbs 22:6
Colossians 3:21
Hebrews 10: 35-38

Unwavering Faith

Start today by showing your love for the Lord by your actions. People can talk, give speeches about how much they love the Lord but when it comes to being a servant for him, they seem to always have more on their plate than they can handle. Take time and make time for the Lord. Do not put him at the end of your list. Put him at the front of your list and make him first in your life.

Do not let anything or anyone stop you from serving him. His love for you is everlasting and his Holy words are the truth! Start listening to the Lord and do what he says. You let him lead you and trust him with all of your heart. Never doubt him! Do not be for the Lord as long as things are going good. Then time trouble come you want to throw your hands up and run. Stay with the Lord, live for him, be like him!

James 1:6-8
Matthew 21:22
Mark 11:22
Matthew 17:20
Luke 17:6

The Slothful

Laziness is not good for anyone. It can drain you of ever wanting to do something with your life. When you make up an excuse not to work or be helpful with chores around the house, it shows that you are trying to avoid responsibility. You are wasting your time when you make excuses for not being helpful. God did not put you here on earth to just lie around and do nothing. If he blessed you with good health where you can walk, use your hands, talk and communicate with people, than you can work! Life is short! Get a move on! Learn as much as you can in life! Do not miss out on all the great things that God has for you to do for him! We all have a purpose for being here on this earth. Ask him what is yours!

Proverbs 15:19
Proverbs 22:13
Proverbs 6:10-11
Proverbs 24:30-31

He is Worth Waiting On

Do you ever wonder will something good ever happen to you? Well something good happen to you each day you are awaken by God. That is a blessing all by itself! He is the one that controls everything. Although, we may live in a world with so much turmoil among us, he manages to keep a smile on our face with his love. He is the one that has his protection all around you when you trust him. Do not think about trying to feel sorry for yourself when all kind of problems come your way! Rejoice and know that God have better things for you coming your way. Praise and acknowledge him for all he has done for you. Wait on him! He is worth waiting for.

Jeremiah 17:7
Psalm 84:12
Psalm 40:4

Peaceful Streams

You know, to reach those peaceful streams you have to be led by the Lord. You cannot just do what you want in life. There are a lot of people that do not ask God anything! You are to seek the Lord in everything that you do. It just shows how you have so many people doing their own thing.

Then when things go wrong or when trouble come THEN they will seek the Lord. Take time to look at nature that is all around you. God created a beautiful world that man is slowly destroying. The Lord is the one that give you tranquility and security in your life when you have a close relationship with him. It shows his Holy love which is the peaceful stream that his spirit brings to give you peace and joy. Acknowledge him, praise him, and let him lead you as you seek him to help you along the way. He loves you and only wants the best for you. He comes with peace!

Psalm 23:2
Psalm 46:4
Ezekiel 34:14

Boast about the Lord, not you!

Tell people about the Lord; how he healed the sick, raised the dead. How he loves you and will forgive anyone of their sins. How he was beaten and bruised and died on the cross so that we all can be saved. Boast and tell everyone about Jesus. Do not go around being proud bragging about yourself. But thank the Lord for all that he has done for you and your family. Let him know how much you appreciate him. You will never get tired of telling people how good God is and how Jesus sacrificed his life for everyone. The glory goes to Jesus, not you!

Psalm 34:2
Psalm 44:8
Psalm 30:12

Do not stick your nose in other people business

Stop being in other people business and examine your own self! Stop wasting your time being nosy. Get real! Sometimes it is best not to say anything or give your opinion when someone asks you a question about someone. When you see how people are having problems and struggling with different situations, pray for them! Some people seem to love to hear any juicy bad news about someone. God gave you life. He want you to use it wisely, not wasting time getting into people business talking about things that will tear them down! Learn how to turn a negative situation into a positive situation. Always tell people about the Lord. Let them know that no matter how bad things are; do not forget about the Lord. The Bible is a book that should be read by everyone. Not sitting somewhere on a coffee table gathering dust! God is the answer for any problem. Pray to him! Praise him! Get to know him!

Psalm 15:3
Exodus 23:1
Psalm 28:3
II Thessalonians 3:11

So you think rap music is the thing!

Be a person to take time and evaluate the product before you follow the leader and jump right in. People that rap on a CD that is being played on the radio get paid for that CD. Teens and adults listen to the words and hear all those awful things that they are rapping about and they see no wrong in it. You cannot go into the world trying to portray the things and become that person that they are rapping about. A gangster with a gun when they kill, they will do time or be killed. You have to care more about your life. Not live in a dream world where you think everything is suppose to be cool with nice cars, expensive homes and name brand clothing with a man or a woman. Those are all material things that will rot away one day. Set your mind on God and his Holy words on how to get to know him and how to make it to heaven. When you change your life to live for the Lord, you will see how he is better than any rap music or anything on this earth!

Psalm 27: 7-8
Psalm 105:4
Acts 1: 12-13

The Comforter

We all live in this world where things are moving fast and you associate with all races of people. You try to keep up with things of this world, mainly material things. People are putting their faith in man and not God! Do not get so caught up in this world where you put Jesus on the back of the list! The Holy Spirit is the comforter that reminds you what Jesus taught and the miracles he did while he was here on earth. It keeps you grounded so you will not go astray. It is a peace that let us know that we do not have to fear tomorrow. Always put God first in your life. Study his words every day. As you seek the Lord, get your friends and relatives to join you in serving the Lord everyday of your life!

John 14:26
John 1:33
John 15:26
John 16:7

Living under Grace

Loving someone is a good thing. To show that you have love in your heart shows that you can actually care for someone. God bless each and every one of us with special gifts to be used toward his kingdom. To love someone enough to tell them about the Lord, spreading the good news about him show that you love him and want to be a servant for him! It shows that you believe in him. God say we are to love one another. Not sit around and find fault on one another, to keep up strife and hate toward each other. Love is the foundation of Grace. God love and he care about everyone, even the sinners. His grace is sufficient for everyone. Keep believing and spreading the good news about the Lord!

Romans 12:6
II Corinthians 12:9
Philippians 4:13

God will forgive all Sin

When you come to the Lord with your sins, you do not have to be ashamed of all the sin that you have committed in your life. Most people feel as if their sin is so harsh that God will not forgive them. But if you ask him to forgive you he will. There is no sin that he will not forgive you for. So many people are living miserable lives not knowing that Jesus loves them so much, that he will forgive them for whatever sin they have committed. Pray to Jesus with a sincere heart. Repent of your sins and start a new life knowing that Jesus loves you! He sees no fault in you!

Psalm 40:12
Psalm 65:3
Psalm 4:3

Love your Enemies

Do not let people get the best of you! When someone hurt your feelings or threaten you and you feel afraid. Shake that fear off of you! *"For God hath not given us the spirit of fear; but of power, and of love, and of a sound mind."* **II Timothy 1:7 KJV** The best way to conquer the enemy is with love. **You have to have a humble and kind spirit.** Put your faith and trust in the Lord! Do not get angry and feel as if you have to take up for yourself. Jesus will be there with you. He is the one that will keep you safe from the enemy. The more you show love, the more the enemy will leave you alone! The enemy will think about it later and realize that it was wrong to be mean to you. Showing love will make you strong with the Lord by your side. Learn how to pray for your enemies and wish them well. You will become a healthier and happy person!

Matthew 5: 43-44
Romans 13:9
Luke 10:27

The Need to Look Good to Fit In

Have you ever thought that you can just be yourself and fit in?! Everyone is unique in their own way with so many different personalities and ways of thinking. This is not hard to do. Just be you and you will see that it will make you a happier person. People will see something beautiful in you that you thought you never had or could imagine. Do not ever feel ashamed of how you look! If you are slim or a healthy full size, be proud of it! God created you in his image. We are to be happy with his Marvelous Creation. We are his **MASTERPIECE!**

Ephesians 2:10
Zechariah 2:8
Deuteronomy 32:10

No Weapon Formed against you will succeed

Keep on doing what you are doing! Have you ever been told by someone that admire the way you look and handle yourself?! People with lovely personalities, great attitudes that just love people and love to smile always get unique compliments. Then here come the enemy that stand on the sideline looking at how you handle yourself and watch as everyone admire you. Jealousy, envy, and misery go together with people that hate on the innocent. The enemy has an awful personality. They cannot stand the sight of you and do not even know you! They are miserable and they will not stop until they try to make you miserable! So the enemy set out to attack you with any and everything that is evil. Do not let Satan stand in your way. Meditate on what the word of God say he will do for you. He says that anything the enemy tries to do to you or say against you will not turn out well. Believe his Holy words! They are the truth!

Isaiah 54:16-17
Psalm 37:10-13
Psalm 62: 2-9, 11,12

To Obey (Do as one is told while under your parents care)

As long as your parents or guardian are the caretaker you are to obey them. They are to have their best interest for you. Every family lifestyle is different with love, problems and God! No family is perfect. When you find yourself beside yourself and you feel as if you are so grown that you do not want to listen to your guardian, go to your Bible. Read what it says about obeying your parents or guardian. Just because a parent or guardian gives you some advice in life about many circumstances that may come up now and then, do not mean not to listen to them! You never get too old to learn something. Be respectful and listen. When you respect your parents it is just like respecting God! God has the answer to all of your problems.

Ephesians 6: 1-3
Proverbs 6:23

Confess Your Sins

Relief comes to all that confess their sin and give their life to the Lord. Many people are out in the world that does not know what to do when things start falling down all around them in their family. Broken homes, troubled marriages, lose their business, owe bills, lose their job, have no money, owe taxes, and have sickness in their body, their only car break down! So many horrible things happening everywhere they turn. What do you do!? Some kill themselves or get on drugs or become an alcoholic or just run away from the problem and end up homeless! I love to tell people about Jesus! He loves you and has never left you. Go to him in prayer. Repent of your sins. Ask Jesus to forgive you for your sins. Talk to him! He is the only one that can put you on the right road. Become a servant for the Lord. Ask him to help you. There is nothing impossible for Jesus. When you change your life to become a servant for the Lord, He will make a way out of no way for you. Put your faith and all your trust in Jesus. He will carry you thru!

Numbers 5:7
Leviticus 5:5
Psalm 66:17-20
Ezra 10:11
Micah 7:18

Do not be too proud to ask for Help

Anytime things in your life start to unravel all around you do not be so quick to give up! Seek the Lord! Everyone have problems and go thru bad times every now and then. Do not be afraid to ask the Lord for help! Do not let a friend or relative stop you from seeking help when things go wrong. Even if you have never tried the Lord, go to him in prayer. He loves everyone and he is always beside you with all power in his hands. Look to him for everything that you need. Do not be afraid. He has nothing but love for anyone that seeks him. He will never fail you!

John 15:7,9
John 3: 35
John 5:20

The Best is Yet to Come

As you study the word of the Lord, it will make you draw closer to him. His words are powerful and true. Whatever problem occurs, the Bible has the answer. Jesus has everything you need. Whether you are happy or sad, he is your way maker. He is your provider. Stay close to him.

When you are lonely or someone has hurt you. When you feel like giving up. Run to Jesus with your tears, your worries, your heartache and pain. He is always there for you. Remember the best is yet to come when you have Jesus in your life!

John 3:16
John 14:21
Romans 5:8

You Learn Something new every day

If you happen to run into someone or know someone that think they know everything and you cannot tell them anything. Please do not get offended! Tell them in a nice way that people learn something new every day! It is good to be knowledgeable about life. But learn also about God who is eternal. Do not get an attitude as if you have heard it all because you have not! Search for the Lord who has all the answers. It is a pitiful thing to think that you know everything. You will at no time ever know everything! God is the only one that knows everything. When you go to the Lord in prayer he can help you with your every need. He knows all about you. He created you.

James 1:5
Proverbs 2: 2-3
Proverbs 13: 13-14
Proverbs 10:14

Surrender to God

Tired of just being tired? Give your life to the Lord. Talk to him and tell him all about your problems. Have you been trying to handle bad situations on your own? Have you been trying to work two jobs and still not getting anywhere further in life? Have you been abused physically and mentally? Are you sick where the doctor gave you up to die? Is there so much bad things going on in your life that you feel like giving up? When all has failed, no matter how hard you try, no matter how much you try to put the best on the outside turn to the Lord! He loves you and is there to help you, always. God say that you have not because you asked not. He will forgive you from all of your sins. Just ask him. Take your crazy thoughts, your illness and anything that is trying to attack you to the Lord; and watch him work!

I John 5:14-15
John 15:5

Diligence, Determination, Discipline

Diligently seek the Lord. You have to have it in your heart to want to learn more about him. Be a servant for him. You have to be determined to please God not man. Have love in your heart for the Lord. Be discipline in wanting to do better with your life. Tell your friends, family and neighbors about Jesus. Let nothing get in your way to try to turn you around. When the love of God is in your heart, nothing will be able to stop you!

Proverbs 12:1
Galatians 1:10
I Thessalonians 2:4
Proverbs 31:17

Make the Lord your Refuge

Putting your faith in the Lord, show the trust you have in him. Your strong faith keep you grounded with no fear, knowing that the Lord has his shield of protection all around you. It is a good feeling to live and know that in times of trouble the Lord will come to help and make the enemy flee. Never let the horrible things of this world put fear in your heart. When God step in to help you, he is there forever, not for a short period of time. Make the Lord your first priority each and every day of your life. His actions show love!

Psalm 46:1
Psalm 91: 9-10
Proverbs 12:21

There is no fear in God's Love

It is a good thing to know that in everything that you do God is present there. He wants you to know that you are definitely safe with him around. God is love! You have nothing to fear. God's love will protect you from evil or anything that try to bring harm to you, or your family or your friends. *"Nothing can separate you from God's love. Not your fears for today or your worries for tomorrow."*-**Romans 8:38 KJV**. Start today by showing God how much you love him. Find time to worship him, pray to him and tell people everywhere you go about him. Be a servant to him and thank him for his many blessings. He has a never ending love for you. Take his love and embrace it!

I John 4:18
Romans 8:39
Zephaniah 3:17

He will order his Angels

When you surrender to the Lord he will keep you safe. No matter where you go in this world, you do not have to fear. When you give your life to the Lord and ask him to protect you, he will. He will do what he says he will do. He is not just blowing smoke and telling you anything! His Holy words are the truth. He wants you to have faith in him with no doubt that he will keep you safe. Even if you are on a plane, at the mall, at work, at school, in a car, on a bus, on a cruise ship, on a roller coaster, in a coal mine, in a submarine, at war, in a hurricane, in a tornado, in a flood, in a wild forest fire or the devil himself try to attack you. He will always have his angels all around you to fight for you. Rest assure, he will protect you!

Psalm 91:11
Matthew 4:6

Be the Best you can be

The Lord wants you to do good in this life. He does not like when evil come around you to stop your progress. Put Jesus in everything that you do. Pray before you do anything. Before you take a test, run track or play any sport, pray. Then do the best that you can. You do not have to be perfect. No one is perfect but Jesus Christ. It does not matter what job you may have, or chores you may have or what schoolwork your teacher may give you. Just be the best you can be. Do not let anyone discourage you. Jesus is the encourager!

Romans 12:8
I Peter 4:10-11

Get your Rest

In this fast pacing world where it feels sometimes as if you are racing with time. Everyone needs to take time to find time for rest. An over worked and tired body is unhealthy. There will always be something to do and places to go. Neglecting yourself to keep up with things in this world will quickly wear you down. Take time to relax in the Lord in prayer. The Sabbath Day should be about praising and thanking God as you rest with him in your mind and heart! Take time to talk to him, and thank him for all that he has done for you and all that he is going to do. Make time for rest! Jesus did.

Genesis 2:2-3
Hebrew 4:4
Exodus 20:11
Exodus 31:17

A friend that stick closer than a brother

You know, being truthful to a person means a lot. When you do what you tell someone, by being dedicated to stick to your words; people feel as if they can trust you. Because you stood good on your word! It does not feel good when someone has promise you something and they never do it. A true friend will go out of the way to help you, to be there for you when problems come, to give you their last. When you hurt, they hurt! Always be that friend that will tell the truth and not a lie! If you see something that you know you will not be able to do to help your friend, tell the truth! They will understand if they are a true friend. Love your friend just like Jesus love you!

Proverbs 18:24
Proverbs 11:30

Stand up to Fear

Do not fear evil people or let fear come upon you to try to quench your loving and kind spirit. Know that every evil scheme end in failure. God will always have the victory! In life, as you get older you will face fear sooner or later. The fears of this world will become hard to bear. This is when you should focus on the Lord even more. Repent of all your sins. Ask God to forgive you and to strengthen you where you are weak. When your peers say things like; you're chicken, you're afraid to try drugs. Do not let fear sink in! Stand up to them without fear! Then tell them how drugs are the work of Satan. That it will only kill, steal and destroy them! Nothing good will happen to you by doing something wrong! Live for the Lord and represent him, not Satan!

Psalm 69:16
Psalm 63:3
Psalm 25:15

Always show respect to elderly people

Anytime you see elderly people, always show respect to them. Do not curse in front of them. Do not push and shove them. They are very delicate. As you get older you will get fragile! Some elderly people bones are easier to break and their walk get shorter. You have to be patient with them. Take some time to observe and just look at them. You can learn a lot from them. Do not disrespect them by trying to impress a friend. Some younger people love to show their bad side around elderly people. If you have a neighbor, a teacher or a church member that is elderly, spend some time with them. They have so much to offer which is great wisdom. Jesus wants us to love and care for everyone, even the elderly!

Leviticus 19:32
I Timothy 5:1-2
Titus 2: 2,6

Set your mind on knowing Christ

If you do not know the Lord, make a list of things that you would like to know about the Lord. When was he born? What did he do while he was here on earth? How long did he live on earth? Why did people hate him? Why was he crucified? There is so much to learn about Jesus. When you dedicate your time to Jesus to study the word you will get close to him where you will learn more and more about him. It is never too late to find him. He is God's messenger. Commit your life to him. Make the Lord your priority. You will not regret it!

Hebrew 3:1
Malachi 3:1
Mark 1:2

Take an Inventory

When you find yourself feeling sorry for yourself. Spend some quiet time to think back on the wonderful things that the Lord has done for you and thank him. If you were to write down each and everything the Lord has done for you, it would surely put a smile on your face and remove the sadness from your heart. Think about how he has blessed your family, friends and you with so many great things that you know you could not have gotten on your own. He shows his love everyday for everyone. Why not take time to praise and thank him! He really, really is entitled to the praise!

Ephesians 5:20
I Timothy 6:8
Hebrew 13:5

Learn to Smile

There is so much to hope for in the Lord. He is the one that has all power in his hand and without him you would not be able to do anything. He is the one that wake you up in the morning. That protect you on the highway, on your job, at school, or wherever you go. He blesses you with money, food, good health, and a peace of mind. When you put God in your life, repent and ask forgiveness for your sins he will make a way out of no way for you. Do not walk around complaining about things that did not go your way. Put God in your life. Smile and know that he love you and will never let you down. When you meditate on his Holy words and think about all he has done for you. It would be very hard not to smile!

Psalm 96:2
Psalm 98:4
Psalm 100:1

There is no one perfect but Jesus Christ

Jesus does not get angry with you when you mess up! He knows that you are not perfect. He wants you to grow strong in learning from when you do wrong, to turn to doing right when you make a mistake. Never feel afraid to ask for forgiveness for your sins. He wants you to be sincere with him. You do not have to be perfect when you ask God to help you. He want the drunkard, the prostitute, the liar, the thief, the adulterer, the stripper, the home wrecker, the wife beater and all sinners to come to him. Do not think that you have to fix yourself up first to come to the Lord. He wants you just as you are because he loves you. Give your heart to the Lord. He wants to save you, to show you the way, to restore you. Do not miss out on Jesus thinking you have to be flawless to come to him! Get help from him just as you are!

Ephesians 5:6-7
Luke 5:32

Run to see what the end is going to be

Do not give up on living for Jesus! As you get closer to the Lord, serving him and telling the world about him, problems will surface to make it hard for you sometimes. But push on forward knowing that the Lord is by your side. Keep working for the Lord. Get stronger and not weak in telling others about him. As you focus on the word of God, trust and believe that the Lord will do what he say about taking care of his people. He will keep you safe from the enemy, from any sickness or disease that try to come upon you. Focus on God and his promises. God is the one that will take care of you. Man will disappoint you. Keep your strong faith in the Lord. Do not be ashamed of him. Keep praising and worshipping him. You will be happy and so thankful that you did!

II Thessalonians 3:3
I Corinthians 1:9
I Chronicles 29:18

The Bible is our Road Map to God

The Bible is one of the best -selling books of all time that are sold in bookstores, and seen in churches and some hotel rooms. Some choose not to read it and is rarely understood by so many. Whenever I go over to someone's home, most of the time I will spot a Bible sitting on the lamp table or on a book shelf in the corner or on a table collecting a lot of dust. You can tell by looking at all the dust on it that no one is reading it. The Bible can help you. It is God's Holy words that were put on the writer's heart from the Holy Spirit. Anything that you want to know about God and his son Jesus can be found in the Bible. The Bible can save your life. It is a guide that should be read every day of your life. Do not pick it up only when sorrow comes and you feel as if you have nowhere else to look for help. Get God's help everyday by reading his Holy words. He is the word! Follow his directions! He will not lead you wrong!

II Timothy 2:15
Psalm 139:10

Stop, Look, Listen

Listen to the sounds. Take time to look at nature, the trees, the birds, and all that God created. Take time to breathe, to think and slow down, and meditate on God's Holy words. It seem as if life today is always rush, rush, rush. Sometimes it feels as if time is passing you by. You have to take some time to spend with Jesus. Find the right place where you can really talk to him and hear what he has to say. You will never go wrong when you follow Jesus. He has the time and patience and love for everyone. He is never in a hurry!

I John 4:16
II Thessalonians 3:5

The Lord is Truly My Shepherd

The Lord is everything you will ever need. He is the one that watches over you. He sees when you are in pain struggling thru life, in need of help, and cannot find your way. When trouble is all around you, he steps in to make things better for you with his angels. He bless you with a safe home with his ever protection. He makes sure that you are in need for nothing because he is your shepherd. It is such a blessing to have Jesus as your helper and guide thru life. Give your all to him. Repent to him and live to worship and praise him. Serve him as you spread the good news about him to everyone! Believe his sacred words that are powerful and will never change. Draw stronger with your faith and trust in him. He will always provide and take care of you! He is your shepherd!

Psalm 23: 1
I Peter 2:25
Isaiah 53:6
Hebrews 13:20-21

Do Not Be a Dropout

Are you happy at school? Do you like your classes? Are you more concern about trying to impress to fit in or your education? Are you being bullied? Are you failing in your classes? Do you think school suck? Are you having problems at home? Do you feel as if no one cares about your future? Do you think you are not dress right for school? Do you think that you are a nerd? Do you just want to be alone? Do you think you are supposed to be working to help your parents or parent at home? Do you think school is not for you? Satan will put all kind of senseless thoughts in your mind, with so many doubts to try to block you from succeeding in life to get an education. Whatever your situation, no matter how bad it is. Take it to the Lord in prayer. He is all about you being the best and doing your best to progress and not fail in life. Let the word **DROP OUT** never find a place in your heart or mind! Let the love of God come into your life that brings Hope, Deliverance, and Victory. God is the way in, not out!

Psalm 139:13-15
Psalm 119:73
Psalm 56:8

If you are angry do not make someone else angry

Some people when they are angry do not feel right until they ruin someone's day by making them angry! Some people walk around with so much hate in their heart and do not know how to ask the Lord to help them. Most people do not believe that the Lord can help them, but he can. If you have a friend or know someone that constantly love to argue. Talk to them. Take the opportunity to tell them about the Lord. How the Lord can heal them and bless them with a peace of mind. Never give up on someone that need help to find their way. You can never assume that everyone know about the Lord! Show your love the same way Jesus showed his love for you!

Proverbs 14:29
Proverbs 16:32
Proverbs 19:11

Do not look any Further

You know, life is funny when trouble comes and you do not know what to do. Especially if you do not know anything about the Lord. It can be like going to a dead end not knowing what to do or which way to go. It is the same way when you are growing up as a teen and you are lost and confused in a world that has so many tribulations. You step out on your own trying to find your way without God in your life. You know, what make life so beautiful is that you have God's son who name is Jesus, that tell people that they do not have to go any further because he is here and has never gone anywhere and has been waiting for you to call on him for so long. Ask God to forgive you of all your sins and give your life to the Lord to cleanse you and show you the way! You do not need to look or go any further because he has been there all the time for you. Are you not still here!?

I John 3:1, 6
John 16:3
John 1:12-13
Romans 8:16

Stay Focus

Your everyday plan is to stay focus. No matter where you are, at home, school, or play. Always know your surroundings, be alert and stay observant. This world has change so much where staying focus is a must because it can save your life. When you put God in your life you will not be afraid as you live your life and go about your daily activities. God want everyone to enjoy life with a peaceful mind with no fear. At school, at the mall, the park, the movies, on the plane or wherever life takes you. Always acknowledge God and know that you will be alright because he is with you. Do not let anyone tell you differently. When God is near and you acknowledge him, Satan will stand back!

Psalm 34:4
Proverbs 1:33
Hebrews 13:6

Never be Jealous of your friends

Live a healthy life by being happy for your friends and fellowman. Do you know that being jealous of someone is not going to change anything? You can be jealous of someone's car, a person's personality, their looks, their home, or anything! It will never make you have what they have. Being happy for them will send all kind of blessings your way. When people spend so much time checking out what another person have, they miss out on what they have. You have something unique about yourself if you concentrate on yourself more. Pray to the Lord and ask him to remove your jealousy and replace it with love in your heart. You have better things to do with your life than to be jealous of someone. Spend it with God. He will show you a remarkable side of you that you thought you never had. Be happy!

James 3: 14-16
Philippians 2:2
I Thessalonians 5:15

The God of all Comfort

When we go to God in prayer, he will give us hope to go on. He let us know that he is always with us and that he see everything and will not leave us unattended where the enemy can tear us apart! The Bible says that; *"When we suffer, Christ suffers with us"* - **Acts 9:4-5 KJV** God is a comforter and he shows us how to handle difficult problems that come our way. He supply us with his Holy words that give us strength and show us how not to run away from bad situations. When a friend is having bad pain and sorrows in their life, do not shy away from them. Run to them to comfort them in their time of troubles. This is how God want us to love and care for one another with strength and not weakness, because he is the comforter!

II Corinthians 1:3-7
Isaiah 51:12

Let God Fight Your Battle

Living this life come with the good and the bad. Some people do not know how to handle the bad. Do not get frustrated when your burdens try to weigh you down. Satan love to try and block your blessings. Keep the best on the outside and steady move forward doing good for the Lord. I do not care what may try to stop you. Never give up! When so many bad things come your way, get stronger in prayer. Sometime it could be that you are doing some good work for the Lord. Jesus said that we would be persecuted for his sake. So rejoice and be happy in the Lord and be thankful to know that he is the one that will fight your battle for you.

Isaiah 49:25
Jeremiah 50:33-34
Psalm 35:1,3

Never be Afraid to Stop Someone from Doing Wrong

Can you imagine how speaking up can save a life sometime!? If you ever see something bad about to happen, always get help! Never be afraid to save a life. If you hear or see someone planning to do something wrong, do not hesitate to stop them. Ask the Lord to be with you and to protect you and he will. The Lord will shield you from any harm that try to come upon you. Whenever you call on the Lord he will come with all the protection you need, which is him! He is the one that has all power in his hands. He is the one that will never make a mistake. He is the one that get things done. Do not get weak with fear all around you. Satan bring fear that will make you afraid to do anything to help. If fear get in your heart, stand strong with your faith and trust in the Lord. Jesus will never leave you alone with the enemy. He is always there with you to keep you safe. When you step up to help, it shows your love for your fellowman!

Mark 6:50
Matthew 28:20

He Will Never Let the Righteous Be Shaken

When you put your trust in God you are not to worry about hardship that may come your way. You are to bring all of your worries to God. Do not waste your time by laying a heavy burden on your heart. Do not be ashamed to show people how much you love the Lord. If you truly trust in God, then trust him to deal with you to grow in grace. He is God! Continue to seek him, to be like him in all that you do. God will never let you down. He will do what he says he will do! Commit yourself to him!

Psalm 37:7
Proverbs 16:3
Proverbs 3:6
I Chronicles 28:9

God Will Rescue You from Every Trap

Whenever you call on the Lord in prayer he will help you. He will even help you in a lot of bad situations when you do not pray. He loves us that much that when he sees you are in trouble, he will come. It is so good to know that we do not have to live in fear. When you have something on your mind that is troubling you, talk to the Lord! There is nothing too complicated for the Lord. He let you know that if you put your faith in him, the enemy does not stand a chance!

Psalm 40; 13-17
Psalm 91:3

Have a Good Samaritan Spirit

What would you do if you came across someone that were having problems at your home, someone at your school or someone that just stayed sad all the time and felt like giving up? Would you pass by unconcern not caring about the person's hardship? The Bible tells us that we are to be concern about our fellowman. That is God's Holy words! Take time to show love and seek to see if there is any way you can help the person. Think about what God would do. Remember to do unto others as you would have them to do unto you. I would hope that it would be something kind and loving! Put others FIRST!

Philippians 2:5
I John 2:6
Matthew 22:39

Love, a by-product

Show the world how you are to live for God. Do it from your heart! God say to love our neighbor! Our neighbor could be anyone. As Christians we should have it in our heart to be loving, have patience, and kindness to everyone. If you say you love Jesus someone you never seen and not have love in your heart for anyone else, this would make it hard for anyone to believe you. It would make you look like a hypocrite. When it comes to other people we are to have joy and love for them. Even when people are mean and cruel to you, always show love. This is the Godly and only way! It is so easy to love others when you have the Holy Spirit inside of you.

Colossians 1:8
I Corinthians 13:13

Afraid of Going to School

I think someone has gone thru the ordeal of being afraid to go to school one time in their life. Afraid of being threaten by the person who start up the trouble. Afraid of being intimidated, stared down and knowing that when the incidents are reported. The teachers are afraid, where nothing is ever done to the perpetrator. Fear is no joke! It can hinder you if you let it. Being afraid can block you from so many blessings if you give in to fear. God want you to bring your problems to him. Fear is like a crippling sickness that will hold you down making you afraid to step out to do anything! Fear is a very uncomfortable thing to carry on your back. Ask the Lord to remove the fear out of your heart and replace it with his love where you can live. Trust and serve him. God's love brings peace and security!

Psalm 34: 5-6
I King 5:4
Genesis 46:3-4

Do Not Feel Unsafe at School

Always know that wherever you go God is there and he has his Holy Angels watching over you. Do you know that feeling afraid is not going to keep you safe!? Do not live with fear in your heart! Do not let anyone intimidate you. Remember, you have the Lord on your side. You are safe anywhere you go if you believe in the Lord and believe that he will keep you safe. God has all power in his hands. You have to know it and truly believe it! When you pray to the Lord and give your life to him. It shows that you trust him to keep you safe!

Romans 8:38
John 10:28

Run to Win the Race

Serving the Lord, being a warrior against the enemy by telling others about the Lord, may cause obstacles to get in your way. But keep being the messenger, strong in the Lord. Never let anything stop you from serving God and telling everyone about him. When you hear people testimonies of how good God has been to them and helped them thru so many difficult situations. They are witnesses of the wonderful things that the Lord has done for them and hard times that he brought them thru. That should make you push harder forward, even stronger to spread the word of God. Whatever it is you love to do that takes you away from serving the Lord, ask the Lord to take that desire away from you and give that time to the Lord! Do not let anything stop you from serving the Lord. You are striving to save a soul; even your own!

Hebrews 12:1-2
I Corinthians 9:24
Philippians 3: 12-13

Remember Your Destination, Heaven

When you find yourself getting weak in faith in the Lord, meditate on all that he has done for you. Meditate on his Holy words. Think about the times he came thru for you. When you think that all is lost in your circumstances, do not get weak and go back to your sinful ways. Stay focus on the Lord. Pray more, study his words (the Bible) more! Do not think about getting weak but anchored in your faith! Your goal is HEAVEN!

Colossians 1:5,12
I Peter 1:4

When Others Try to Break Your Spirit

You know you are doing right by God when people are attacking you on every side and around every corner. The Bible says that you will be preyed upon by Satan as you get closer to God. But be ready to take it by not giving up. Prayer changes things. Smile at the situation that you are going thru and know that your redeemer lives. He is right by your side. Pray for the one that are giving you a hard time. Stay tough and keen in the Lord, never lacking strength. It is so good to know that when you call on the Lord he will come!

Psalm 70:1
Psalm 71:24

Put Others First

Love is an action word that can show more than what is said. When you see a friend or anyone that seem to have something bothering them, step up to see what is upsetting them and be genuine in offering your help. A kind word or a helping hand could save a life. Show your love, be caring about someone else. Put them first and do it from your heart! If you think about what Jesus would do, your actions will always turn out right. He loves everyone and you should too!

I John 3:16-17
John 13:1

Hold to God's Unchanging Hand

When your friends and love one turn their back on you, do not give up on them. Continue to love them and pray for them. You never know what a person is going thru. Most people when they are having problems in their home, at school, on their job, with a friend or loved one, will keep it to themselves. They could have so much pain built up inside of them that they do not know how to handle it. Never forget about Jesus! Tell everyone about him. Know that the Lord will never let you down. He will never disappoint you. Tell everyone how his love is everlasting and that what he says he will do, he will do. His precious words will stand forever! Live to be like him. He is the same yesterday, today, tomorrow and forever!

**II John 6
Psalm 36:7
Psalm 139: 17-18
Psalm 91:4**

Let Your Love Shine Through to Others

When you smile and have a happy spirit, people everywhere will want to be around you. When you have God in your life he will give you that glow. But beware! Satan will try to break your spirit. Do not let him. Always be pleasant, nice and kind to others! The best way to handle a person that try to give you a hard time is to be kind to them. The harder they are on you, the nicer you are to them! Do not let that person bring you down to their level. Keep the love of God in your heart and shine, shine, shine! Let the light in you shine and give God the glory.

Ephesians 5: 8-9
I Peter 2:12

My Soul Has Desired You

Take time to go to church to praise the Lord and to learn more about him. If you can go out to a party, take time to go shopping at the mall, or take time for a group of friends or family members, you can take time for God! When you take time to study the word of God it will help you to get to know God better. The more you study it will bring you closer to him. "My soul is consumed with longing for your laws at all time."- Psalm 119:20. Seek to get closer to the Lord.

Psalm 43:4
Psalm 84: 1,2 4
Psalm 27:4

When the Enemy Attack You

Think about what Jesus would do in a situation like this! It is hard for some people to control themselves when people are out to attack and hurt them for telling others about the Lord. But the same God that spoke to Abraham, Moses and Noah is alive today. He has never left us and he is not going anywhere. Do not be ashamed of him. He will always be here to help you. If you do not love him and believe in him and acknowledge him, then it would be as if you do not need him or want to know him. God is always ready to help. Repent of your sins. Reach out to him and he will be there for you! Learn how to rejoice in suffering that will only strengthen your trust in God.

Matthew 5:12
Hebrews 11: 32-38

His Love is all around us

You can just take time and look at God's creation all around you and notice the love. The magnificent earth that he created with the beautiful trees, awesome streams, the sea, ocean, breathtaking hill sides and mountains; the moon and stars at night, and the sun and floating clouds that seem to watch over us all thru the day and some clouds at night! The rich land that supply your food and clothing. What love! He shows you how you do not have to want for anything because he is the one that provides your every need. The artwork designed on every animal, and creature great and small. He took the time to create everyone and everything. Whenever you are feeling sad, take time to step outside and look in the directions of the East, the West, the North and the South and admire the atmosphere. Then thank God for loving you and creating you and this world. You have something to be thankful for; you are alive and you have God. If you do not know him! Get to know him! HE LOVES YOU!!!!!!

Psalm 107:1
Psalm 136:1-9
Hebrews 12:28

Fire Goes Out Without Fuel

Hearing gossip can be juicy when you do not have God in your heart. When you have the love of God in your heart, you do not have time to sit around and talk (gossip) about anyone. Spreading rumors, telling lies, causes so much trouble. When someone tell you that this person said this or that about you, have no comment. This is how Satan love to get things started and heated up! Pray for the person and move on. When you do not feed into the negative conversation it will not go anywhere. When someone is trying to argue with you, it will die down if you do not have anything to say. Learn how to control your tongue in what you say about someone and when it comes to someone arguing with you. Ask the Lord to give you the strength and to change your ways. If you do not have anything good to say about someone, do not say anything! A quiet mouth is peace and a loud mouth is TROUBLE!

Proverbs 16:28
Proverbs 24:28
Proverbs 25:18

Praise God

Make an effort to Praise the Lord every day. Think about all he has done for you. Even when things did not go your way, and you were feeling down, Praise the Lord anyway! Let him know that you love him, that you thank him for watching over you, fighting your battle for you and for making a way out of no way for you so many times. If you have friends that do not know the Lord, tell them about him. Do not let them go another day without knowing the Lord. He is truly worthy to be praise.

Psalm 106:1-2
Psalm 117

Stand in Boldness for Jesus

Never get afraid when the enemy comes around saying bad things about the Lord. Fear is from Satan and love is from God. Satan will attack the weak that has fear in their heart. Stand strong on God's Holy word's knowing that his words are the truth and very powerful and he will come thru for you in any problem that come your way. God want strong warriors that will fight for him. You do not have to ever be afraid to talk about the Lord in front of anyone. Tell your friends about him. Tell strangers about him. Tell everyone in the world about him! Be a servant for the Lord and be all you can be for him and never give up. Get busy! Go spread the message!

Ephesians 6:14
I Thessalonians 5:8
Isaiah 49:2
Jeremiah 23:29

The Praise of a Tree Clap

Trees know how to praise the Lord. Have you ever just stood and watch the trees as the wind blow thru them. It is as if they are swaying their limbs like praising the Lord. It is such a marvelous and awesome thing to watch. This is how I look at trees as the wind blow thru them. It is as if the trees show how they love the Lord as they keep saying thank you with every limb that sways. It is the same thing with a person that have a close relationship with the Lord. They are on a mission! They have a passion, a strong desire to be a servant for the Lord. This is how we should show our love for the Lord and for everyone with a peaceful and joyful heart!

Isaiah 55:12
I Chronicle 16:33

God's Holy Words Are for Everyone

Do not think that you have to be a certain age to learn about the Lord. The earlier you learn about Jesus will help you thru life. God's words, (the Bible) are for protection and guidance and for everyone to learn about him. Get to know him by seeking him with everything in you. Put him first in your life before anything or anybody. Let his words dwell in your heart. His words are powerful and should be read by everyone. Do not be a person that be turned away from the Bible because of someone you know that do not love the Lord. Check Jesus out for yourself. He is all about undying love!

II Timothy 3:15
Isaiah 54:13

Do Not Cling to Anxiety

Learn how to enjoy life by living for Jesus and let go of your sinful ways. Learn how to trust in him and go to him in prayer and leave all your concerns right there. Do you know that worrying about your problems is not going to make things get better!? Go to the Lord, read his Holy words, talk to him! When your enemies are all around you, it is easy to worry when you do not know what to do. Stress and ulcers come from worrying and so many other things that can put you in bad health! Satan do not want you to know anything about Jesus. Satan wants to destroy you. He knows that Jesus is the one that can make everything alright and turn you away from sin. When you put your faith and trust in Jesus, there will be no need to worry. You can have a peace of mind. Make Jesus your choice today!

Genesis 21:7
Matthew 10:19-20
Luke 12:11-12
Luke 12: 25-34

There is Only One God

Think about all that the Lord has done for you all of your life. He has never left you. He will help you when you least expect it! He is an awesome and loving God. We are to acknowledge him and be ready to serve him at any time. There are so many things that people have made their God! Those are the things that you **cherish** more than God. You all know what it is. The things of this world are just that, things! You will never be able to take them with you when you die. There is nothing in heaven you can buy with money. It is best to put your trust in God. When you repent and ask God to show you the way, he will! You are in good hands with him because he is not going anywhere. *"He is the first and the last. The beginning and the end."* - **Revelation 22:13 KJV**. He is our all in all. He is GOD!

Isaiah 43:10-13
Hosea 13:4

Praise God Everyday

Do you know that you can praise God in a song, with an instrument, and even a dance? Have you notice when you sing a song, or play an instrument, it can be so relaxing? This is the kind of healthy spirit that you should stay connected to in your daily life. Praising God is showing how much you love him. It also shows him how grateful you are and that no one can ever take his place! So when you praise him, give him all you got and that is nothing but true love for him!

Psalm 150
Hebrews 13:15

Freely Give To Others

God want you to love him and people more than money. He wants you to feel good spreading the good news about him and to stop worrying about money all the time. The more you give, the more God will give to you. When you help others that do not have, God's blessing will come to you, with money or in a healing for you and your family. All you have to do is be a cheerful giver and politely share what you have with others. Look for people that are in need - The poor, the widowers, and the homeless. When you look out for them, God will look out for you!

Acts 20:35
Leviticus 27:33
Proverbs 3:9-10

Caring For the Poor

I remember a long time ago when someone lost their home from a fire. Everyone in the neighborhood would pitch in to help them get back on their feet. Time has change so much where people do not jump and help each other like Jesus say we should do. When God bless you with financial blessings, you are to look out for the poor and needy. There are many selfish people in the world that do not see it that way. Be obedient to God's Holy words. Instead of dwelling on what all you can buy for yourself! Think of ways you can bless someone in need that really need help!

Deuteronomy 14: 28-29
Deuteronomy 24:19
Job 29:12
Job 34:28

Loneliness

Do not take loneliness as a negative but use it as a positive to spend time with the Lord. You will find that as you get closer to the Lord. It may seem lonely sometimes because some of the friends that you once had will slowly fade away as your faith grow stronger in the Lord. When others seem to fail you, God is always there to lift you up. Always remember, seek the Lord while you can find him! You are never alone. When loneliness and problems try to creep in on you. Draw nearer to the Lord. He has an everlasting love for you. He will never disappoint you!

Psalm 62:1
Psalm 55:22
Psalm 34:18

Missionaries Provide Ministry

The talent that God has blessed you with is to be used to serve God. When you serve and help others it is just like helping God. Everyone has a ministry that they need to pursue. Are you an encourager? Do you lift people spirits up when they are down and feeling low? Do you love to help people that are in need? Do you give to the poor and help the elderly? If you are a loving and kind person that uses your time and efforts to help others, then you are a missionary in your own way, you show how much you love God by the way you have respect for others. Continue to work for the Lord in your daily ministry, loving and caring for others.

I Timothy 4: 12-16
II Timothy 1:6
Matthew 24: 45-46

Stand on God's Word

Sometimes friends can be the main one that talks negative when you decide to change your lifestyle of hanging out with the wrong crowd. The coming in late at night and just doing what you want, not listening to your parents and you know it is wrong. You know it is time to follow Jesus when you see that everything that you have tried to do good on your own is failing and not going right. The more you try to change your life for the better, the more things seem to go wrong for you with bad things happening all around you. Satan is the one that do not want you to get closer to the Lord. He is the one that keep interfering, trying to make it difficult for you to seek God's help. Ask the Lord to fight your battle for you. Tell him that you need him. Read your Bible and ask the Lord for understanding of the Bible. You will see how powerful his Holy words really are!

Luke 21:17-19
Matthew 10:31

Never Put Yourself Down

This is something that so many people do and that is put themselves down. I had a very bad habit of thinking that I had a big nose when I was young growing up. I thought I was so ugly! I had very low self- esteem. This kept me from being happy when I was at school around other kids. I was concentrating on which kid was going to laugh at my big nose and my country name "Maryjane"! It terrified me all the time at school! I read in the Bible where it said that God love us all no matter what we look like. I heard a teacher say that a person can be beautiful on the outside with a nasty personality on the inside. I ran across so many people that were like that in school. I was blessed with a beautiful personality that made me look good from the inside out. I give praises to our Lord and Savior Jesus Christ. If you want to be bless with a peace of mind and love. Find Jesus, he has it all!

Lamentations 3:32
Psalm 119:41
Psalm 119:76

The Right Road

Meeting and getting to know your peers at school and in life, is a challenge in itself. You have so many different people in the world. You have some that believe in doing the right thing and some that love to take chances. Then you have some that believe in doing nothing but horrible things! But in everything that you do there is a lesson to be learned. The road that takes chances is scary to some people. You stole, lied, and did so many things that you were ashamed of and almost got caught! The road to horrible things is a dead end for sure. It scared you to do the right thing for a little while. You went out to destroy at any cost no matter who you hurt. You are selfish and everything is all about you and what you want! You do not care for anyone. The road to rightful things is a healthy path. When you follow the right road you put others first. You seek to live like Jesus. You love people, not material things. You have peace and joy in your heart where you want only the best for people. Not be out to destroy them any chance you get. Study God Holy words. Meditate on them, then let God show you how to get on the right road!

Luke 15:10
Luke 15:18
Psalm 51:4

Street Smart Sense

Each time you walk out the door and enter the world you are to be observant of your surroundings. Whether you are at a sport event, the mall, grocery store, park, airport, beach, school, your neighborhood or wherever you go, be watchful of everything around you. There is so much happening in the world, any and everywhere you go. Pray before you leave your home. Pray while you are at work and before you leave work. Ask the Lord to protect you with his Holy angels all around you. Ask him to protect you from any harm or danger as you step out in the world. Do not live in fear but be smart enough to observe enough to know if evil do come your way; you will know how to run the enemy with God precious Holy words that are so powerful!

Isaiah 25:4
Isaiah 32:2
Psalm 91:1-2
Psalm91:10, 15,16

Celebrate Sundays by Saying Thank You

You know, when God has been so good to you, it make you think about all he has done for you. It should make you want to thank him every day! You wonder where do you begin to thank him for all of the blessings he has bestowed upon you. Start with thanking him for his protection over you all thru the night and for waking you up this morning. Thank him for your school and thank him for your job. Thank him for blessing you with food to eat, clothes to wear and a home. Thank him for your family and the joy you have in your heart. Thank him for blessing you with good health, good neighbors and nice friends; and if you happen to have one that is trying to give you a hard time, thank him for that also. Maybe the one that has lost their way and do not know the Lord may decide to change their life and seek Jesus. Kindness sometime can have a strong effect on an unkind person. Take the day to rejoice and just thank the Lord! Thank him! Thank him! Thank him!

Psalm 92:1-6
Psalm 148

Self-Righteousness

Always be thankful to God for all your blessings. Acknowledge him, giving him the praise because without the Lord you cannot do anything. He is the one that breathe life into your body. He is the one that keep you together and calm when you take a test. He is the one that help you on your job and at home with your chores. He is the one that keep you safe on land, sea and in the air. Never think that you do not need the Lord. All of your blessings come from him. As he blesses you, learn to love others. Do not think that you are better than anyone else. Do not hate them. Always be willing to listen, to learn, to advance. You will never know everything and you will never be perfect. Only Jesus Christ is perfect!

Luke 18: 11-14
Matthew 23:12

Ask God to be with you in everything that you do

Be content and happy with the Lord by your side. When you walk with the Lord and meditate on all that he says he will do for you and how he will protect you. How can you live with fear in your heart? Do not be afraid to live. When you are at school, on your job, at home, or shopping or on vacation, be content! When you pray to the Lord and ask him for protection around you and your family. He will always come thru for you if you trust him and never doubt him. You will feel his presence all around you. Grow in faith and always know that he love you. Show your faith and not live in fear! Receive his blessings and live serving the Lord!

Proverbs 19:23
Numbers 6:24
Genesis 15:1
Psalm 3:3

You who are heavy Laden

Now, are you ready to give your life to the Lord? Have you had enough of the enemy beating you down in everything that you do? Are you tired of getting nowhere? Are you tired of being depressed? Are you tired of getting sick from worrying so much? How much hurt and pain do you have to go thru before you surrender to the Lord? Why are you taking so long to go to him? He is waiting! He wants to help you! He loves you, really love you! Do not let anyone tell you wrong! God has love for everyone but he is not going to make you follow him. This is a choice you have to make. Do not stay with Satan. Get away from him! He is the one that bring all this pain and sorrow to you. Go to Jesus! Confess all of your sins and ask for forgiveness. Jesus is waiting with open arms to help you. Run to him!

Jeremiah 6:16
John 14:15

Be Glad to Serve the Lord

Just talking to the Lord is awesome! Have you tried it! Looking back at all the Lord has done for you, how can you not serve him? You should be happy to do anything for the Lord. When you are obedient to his Holy words and you are out in the world telling people about him is a part of serving the Lord. When you take time to listen to people problems and pray for them is showing that you are serving the Lord. Try to talk to someone each day about the Lord and save a soul! Know that what you are doing is serving the Lord by spreading the good news about him. Never be ashamed of him! Your fellowman might laugh and make fun of you but delight and get even stronger in God's Holy words. This is not about you! It is about God!

Psalm 100:2
Psalm 107:2

Do Not Judge Others

Finding fault in someone is something that a whole lot of teenagers experience in school. Although this can happen to anybody anywhere. This is a tender area that causes so many problems between teens because of one thinking they are better than the other person. Jesus tells us not to judge others. But people will tear an individual down in order to make themselves look good. Before looking down on someone, check yourself! Be ready to fix yourself and to help your peers.

Matthew 7:1-2
James 4:11-12

Stop wasting Your Time Here on Earth Doing Nothing (Do something good for the Lord)

Time is precious and something you cannot go back and get. Every second, minute, hour and day should be used very wisely because you do not know how long you have here on earth. In everything that you do you should acknowledge the Lord because he is the one that love us and keep his promise to us that he will never leave us or forsake us. He is the one that is always there for us. If you have not found Jesus, please seek him today. He is the joy and peace that is missing in your life. Learn about him, then go out and tell the world about him. Look out for the poor, homeless and widowers that is going thru hard times in their life. Be a cheerful giver; have love in your heart for everyone. Love your enemies and pray for them. Do not let anyone steal your joy. Remember, time is very valuable. Spend it with the Lord and meditate on helping people in this life that need help and tell them about Jesus.

II Corinthians 6:2
Titus 2:7
Psalm 72:12

Why Wouldn't You Trust in the Lord?

Have you been up against the wall with so many stumbling blocks in your way and no matter what you do things seem to get worse? Have you tried things your way listening to friends and family members that do not know the Lord? Do you feel as if you are stuck in a rut where nothing good is happening for you? There is nothing good about being sad and disappointed. When is enough, enough? Start a new life serving the Lord. Put your trust in him and live for him. Aren't you tired of doing things your way and not getting anywhere? Give all of your worries to the Lord and put your faith in him! Put your heartaches behind you by trusting in the Lord!

John 15:5,7,8
I John 5:12-13

Search the Scriptures

I tell everyone to read God's precious Holy words and remember them. To check out everything that someone tell you about God. People have been known to change the words of the Bible to what and how they want to portray it. That is a very dangerous thing. God words are sacred and so true. No one is to change any word or saying of what God said. The Bible is a guide, a road map to how we are to live and love one another. We are to follow his directions and the path that he led for us. The Bible is a powerful tool that Satan does not want anyone to know about. Read God Holy words, meditate on them. Let God Holy words be a blessing to you that will remain in your heart forever!

John 5:39
Acts 13:27
Luke 24:27

Did You Ever Consider Asking Jesus

I want to ask you something. Are you tired of not getting anywhere in life? Does it feel as if the more you try to move forward something always pull you backward where you never succeed? Do you have days where everything always goes wrong? Do you have a bad attitude from all of the frustration and problems around you? Do you have Jesus in your life? Do you know him? Do you want to know him? Did you know that Jesus can help you with anything? All of these trials and burden you had to endure is something that Jesus can help you with. He can change your life if you just believe in him. All you had to do was ask him. You can talk to him when you cannot talk to anyone else. He will listen!

Luke 11:9-10
I John 3:21-22

All Teens Do Not Cause Trouble

Many extraordinary teens go to school to try to get an education. They enjoy every minute of school! Then there are some that prefer to be by themselves that really dread school. They have to tolerate being around some that go to school just to cause disturbance. The teens are stereotyped when they walk in a group or a bunch with their peers, that's labeled as the routinely trouble maker. If you were to observe the teens at school in action, you would see how different they are. Some really want to achieve and get their education. Although these different personalities are at school, you have to have a mind of your own and know who to associate with, in and out of school. School has been known by some people, as a place to pick up bad habits from other students. Although all of these things are in your midst, you have to know when to walk away from trouble. Learn to have the Lord in everything that you do; your walk, your talk, your mind, your heart, especially your thinking. Trouble is so easy to get into. Seek the Lord and live for him. Be obedient to his Holy words, in how he says you are to live and love one another. Repent of your sins and always do the right thing in life for the Lord!

Nehemiah 1:5
Acts 5:29

Take Time for Jesus
(Warning and teaching)

Everyone needs to hear the good news about our Lord and Savior Jesus Christ. Without Jesus in your life you will be lost in a world of sin. You will be like a sheep among wolves. It will be just like when a teenager do not want to hear from their parent or guardian what is right and what is wrong. They just want to step out in the world and do their own thing. Without Jesus in their life, it would be just a matter of time before Satan step in and snatch them up, headed toward a road of ruin. Salvation is obtainable to anyone who believes and has faith in Jesus Christ. There is nothing out there in the streets. What you see on the television, is a dream world in movies, with actors that get paid for making all types of movies. Jesus is real and he love you and only want the best for you. He proved it by showing that he died on the cross for all our sins. He does not want bad things to happen to you. He wants you to believe and trust in him and have faith. He wants to save you from destruction.

Colossians 1:28-29
Ephesians 4:13

If you are in a Gang, Get Out!

Do not ever think that by joining a gang that makes you a big person because it does not. Do not let anyone scare you into joining a gang. When you take someone's life - that is a life taken that you cannot give back. Do not do something that will haunt you for the rest of your life. You were not created by God to just live here and die. We all have a purpose for being here in this world. Does a gang help the poor? Do they give food to the needy? Do they bring peace in the neighborhood? Do they help the elderly and widowers with their wants and needs to survive in this world? Do they go to church on Sunday? Attend prayer meetings, or Bible study? Do they donate food and money to the homeless? Do they have love in their heart for their fellowman? What does this tell you? People in a gang are hurting. They have a hurt in their heart where it looks like anything makes them angry and they are out to hurt others. What feel so good about pain? We are to have love in our heart for everyone. You were not put here on this earth to hate people. You can love people but dislike their evil ways. If you know someone that is in a gang, tell them about a man name Jesus that loves them no matter what they have done. He will forgive them for their sins if they ask him! Let them know that the right way in life is following the Lord not Satan! God will give them a peace of mind with love for everyone. Satan will lead them straight to hell! Come to Jesus. Be a servant for him. He will gladly show you the way!

Proverbs 28:13
II Corinthians 7:11

His Name is Jesus

Heartbreak can be something else, especially if you are the one that is being targeted. Tired of people lying to you, using you and talking behind your back? Smiling in your face pretending to be your friend and stabbing you in the back with lies? Aren't you fed up looking for that perfect person? Do you feel as if you have no one in this world that understand you or care about you? Well, you are not the only one! People everywhere is tired of going thru the same pain over and over again that can slowly tear you apart inside. So many people are looking for that perfect person, and you know what!? People are always going to have their faults and excuses! There is no perfect person but Jesus Christ! He is the only one that can be true to you. Ask him to come into your heart. Tell him how much you want to know him and love him. He will give you the love and peace you are looking for and he will never walk away from you. Repent of your sins. He will never lie to you or pretend to be your friend. He is real and his words are the truth. So if anyone ever asks you have you found the perfect one that love you unconditionally and will never hurt you or deceive you. Tell them yes you have found him and his name is Jesus!

II Corinthians 1:3-5
John 15:9-11
John 17:13

Different Nationalities

In school you meet all kind of people. Different race, language, color attitudes and characters. We are to love everyone. This should come natural but for many it does not. God say to respect and love foreigners as you would your own native. Love should have no limit whatsoever. It is to be given and shown to all. Do not fail to appreciate them. Make them welcome by your kindness that we should have for everyone. Show your love. Remember God love EVERYONE. He is not picky!

Romans 15:5
Leviticus 19:33-34
Ephesians 2:19

Save a Soul

When you tell your friends and family about the Lord, you express your love for him. By taking the time to study his words, work for him as a missionary and doing all you can for the Lord show your dedication. Your mission is to try to save as many souls as you can and show how truly committed you are to him. Your actions are showing how much you care about others. Let your love and passion shine for the Lord so that it will be a blessing to everyone you meet. Tell everyone near and far about the Lord and save a soul!

Psalm 91:14
Jeremiah 16:19

Go to School to Learn, Not to Impress!

Many people at school have wasted so much time in life trying to impress someone. That impression is just a show. Do not be so concern about the clothes people wear or their hair style or tattoos! As long as your clothes are clean and pressed, you are good to go. Your clothes will not earn you an "A". Your hairstyle will not help you pass a test and your tattoos will not help you on the track team. Concentrate on what is important in school and college and that is education. You will never be able to impress or satisfy people no matter how hard you try. Ask the Lord to strengthen your mind to learn and not worry about trying to impress. Jesus is a healer and a Savior. Look to him to guide you and to help you!

I Thessalonians 5:11
Philemon 1:20

What is Your Purpose Here on Earth?

This is a good question to ask some of your peers. Get together with some family and friends and talk about it. Anyone can find their purpose here on this earth when they ask the Lord. This is something that you really need to talk to the Lord about because he knows your purpose. When I was growing up at home with my family, no one told me that I was chosen by God with a purpose for being here on earth. We are not here to just live and then we die. Life can be wonderful when you live for the Lord. When you read the Bible ask the Holy Spirit to give you the understanding. It is good to know that God has something special for us to do for him. We are God's workmanship.

Ephesians 2:10
Proverbs 19:21

Pray together and Comfort One Another

There are many single parents that have a teenager somewhere working trying to help the parent make ends meet at home. I think that is a beautiful thing because it shows the love that the child have for the parent. I just want to encourage you to keep keeping on. God will bless you for showing love and for giving your all. If the journey seems to get hard and if you ever feel like giving up, do not! Make sure the communication between you and your parent stay close, to know how things are going on in your lives. Learn how to pray together because prayer is strong. Learn how to comfort one another. You will draw strength from each other. Always keep God in everything that you do and thank him for your many blessings!

Philippians 4:7
Luke 18:1

Rivers of Living Water

Anyone can repent and ask the Lord to forgive them of their sins. You have to make that choice. No one is going to demand that you get saved. God is the fountain of life and the living water. *"God say that to all who are thirsty, he will give with no cost the springs of the water of life"*. - **Revelation 21:6 (KJV)**. If you are heartbroken with sorrow, remember God's promise of complete protection and relief. You can come to God and be saved. Have faith in God with the courage to help others that are not saved!

Isaiah 55:1-2
Revelation 22:17
Lamentation 5:4

Instead of Bullying, Show Love!

Why would anyone want to bully anyone? How is bullying someone going to help you? No one deserves to be bullied! Bullying is something evil from Satan. Anytime someone goes around preying on the kind, humble and smart person to make their life miserable is a sin that come directly from Satan. God is about love and everything that is good. If you just happen to be a bully that is hurting on the inside and is sad and you hate yourself and everything in the world. Seek help! God love you with all your faults. He will never turn you away. Ask him to forgive you for your sins. How would you feel if someone in your family was bullied? Change your life for the best with God in it, by showing love and concern for people. Try to love people; not destroy their lives with hate that you have in your heart. Try being kind and considerate. Do know that what you give to others will one day come back to you!

Psalm 103:8
Psalm 130:3-4

Be Obedient

During these difficult times, life will have some ups and downs where you will be preyed upon. As a teenager you will be tested among your peers. Stay focus on what is right and good. Always be obedient and stand on what God precious words say. Ponder the scriptures. Conduct oneself out of devotion and obedience to God. Set a good moral example of how to live and serve the Lord. Show your love!

Psalm 34:8
I Peter 1:14
Exodus 24:7
Isaiah 1:19

Lord, what do I hope for?

Your hope should be in the Lord. He will be with you as you spread the gospel truth. Do not let any doubt stop you from approaching your peers about Jesus. He will go with you. He will not leave you as you serve him to save a soul. He will help you when others will not. He will be with you at school, in the classroom, courtroom, hospital, at home, or in the streets when your enemies are all around you. He is the one that you put your trust and hope in. He will always help you. All you have to do is call on him. With faith you can have what you need to serve him.

Isaiah 41:10
Romans 8:31

So you lied to someone!
Now tell the truth!

Telling the truth is always the best thing to do. When you lie, it places a burden on you that hang with you. It tears at your body with hope that no one will ever find out that you lied! It is awful to have to live that way. Jesus wants you to live in peace not fear. That thing called 'fear' comes from Satan. He is the one that put you in that predicament of lying in the first place. Then he turn around and laugh at you after he see how much pain he has cause. Now to get away from all of that stress is to simply tell the truth! Ask God to be with you and to forgive you for telling a lie. He will not let any harm come to you and he will comfort you and show you the way. Put your trust in him. Let him bring peace into your life!

Zechariah 8:17
Ephesians 4:25

God's Grace, Love and Mercy

So many times you may have wondered how you were saved from bad things that could have happen to you. It was only by God's grace that you were protected. When you do wrong God will help you find your way. He will give you a chance to get it right. When he forgives you, do not feel as if you can keep sinning because he loves you. God has an undying love for you." His grace is sufficient"! II Corinthians 12:9. His love is real. His mercy endureth forever. Give thanks to the Lord each and every day for having him in your life. Be thankful that he does not look at your faults. Pray for that kind of love that God has for everyone! "Let us therefore come boldly unto the throne of grace that we may obtain mercy, and find grace to help in time of need."- Hebrews 4:16

Ephesians 2:4-6
Hebrews 4:16
Romans 5:20
Romans 7:12

Eternal Perspective
(Life)

People are not to overlook God and be about gaining money, power and fame. We are to live in this world but not be of this world. This world is our temporary home. We are to live each day getting to know Jesus, with a close relationship with him and to prepare our life to live eternally in heaven with him. All the material things and this world are going to pass away. We are to think about eternity. No one knows what tomorrow may bring. People are to make goals that include God everyday of their lives.

James 4: 13-15
Proverbs 27:1

Flourish like Palm Trees

Those who put their trust in the Lord can stand strong on his Holy words; they will not be moved. No matter how bad your circumstances, keep your faith in God. Most of the time when things keep going bad in a person's life, they might feel like giving up. Concentrate on what God words say and believe him! His words are loving, kind, and the truth! Stay strong in your faith for the Lord and keep trusting in him. He will carry you thru!

Psalm 92: 12-13
Psalm 54:7

Do not worry about Tomorrow

Why worry about tomorrow and waste your time when you know you cannot change things? It will only put stress on your body and make you unhealthy. Worrying is something that will bring sickness to your entire body. Every time you worry, you are slowly tearing yourself down. God do not want you to go thru life worrying about anything! When you lean on what the word of God says and believe on him, you will find that he will take all your problems away from you. Worrying is a bad habit to pick up. It makes you lose faith in God. Take all your problems to the Lord. Pray instead of worrying. It is such a great relief when you pray. It reassures you that your troubles will be taken care of. Learn to depend on God and not yourself!

Matthew 6: 25-27
Matthew 6: 34

Pursue God

You would live a better life if you put God first in your life. It is so easy to be kind, to be considerate, to smile, to be happy when you have God in your life. God is all about love and saving souls. Stop cursing, stop lying, stop stealing, and stop thinking it is all about you! It is about God and how he wants us to love him with all our heart and soul. How he want you to love the poor, the widowers and the needy. It is time to get real with God. Pursue God and PEACE!

Psalm 34:14
I Peter 3:11
Matthew 7:7-8

Sinful People

If you are a Christian, obedient to God's Holy words then that is good. You are showing that you believe in the Lord and you love him. This message is for people that see nothing as being sacred. They pollute what is Holy, have no respect for anyone, plus they have evil in their heart.

Those individuals can be saved! We are to seek sinful people living in sin to tell them about the Lord. God's rule of conduct is for anyone who are sexually immoral, perform habitually homosexuality, and are liars and murderers. People who be inconsistent with the moral well being teaching of God's Holy words, do not change what God words say in the bible. This has been done by many, plus homosexuals. If they have read the bible, they know that homosexual behavior is a sin! No getting around it! The bible say to condemn their practice but not them! We are to have love and forgiveness in our heart for them; to pray that their life be converted. Hold your arms open with love and not with judgment. Someone out there needs you to show them the way to the Lord. Be the first to step forward with much love, and that is God!

I Timothy 6:3
II Timothy 4:3
II Timothy 3:1-2

Do not be a Perpetrator of Crime

Getting in trouble, committing a crime is not cool. There is more to life than going to jail. Do not let your friends fool you by making it look like being in jail doing time is the thing. I have worked in the prison system and detention center with the juveniles and believe me it is not cool or the place to be. God has a purpose to why we are here on earth. No one seems to take the time to find out about God and his son Jesus. No one wants to hear about him until they get into trouble. Take time to get to know him. Pick a quiet private area with just you so you can talk to him. Stop wasting your life doing crimes and evil acts that will destroy you. Time is something you cannot get back and a life is something you cannot give back. Give up your old life with Satan, and start a new life with the Lord!

Job 31:33
Ezra 10:1
Daniel 9:4

Frustration, Failure, Fear
(The three F's)

Every day you hear how some teens are frustrated at school. Some feel as if they cannot fit in or understand what is being taught. Some see themselves as failures because the least little thing that give them a problem, make them want to quit and give up! Then fear move in clinging tightly to try to shut them down completely. But that is when you get strong and turn to the Lord. Never quit when the going gets tough! When what you are doing get hard, you know you are doing something right because nothing good comes easy! Pick up the bible, meditate on his Holy words, pray to the Lord, and ask him to forgive you for your sins. He will step in with his arms wide open, willing and able to help you. Your frustration will turn into happiness. Your failure will turn to success. Your fear will turn to power and love. Trust God completely at all times!

Ecclesiastes 7:8
James 1:19
Proverbs 14:29

I Thirst for you

When you feel like you are alone, reach out to Jesus. Diligently seek him. Focus on God's words. Spend time studying his words. The more you study, the more you will want to know about him. He is genuine and worthy to be praise. He is not a character in a fictional story. He loves you and will never abandon you. He is always ready to come to your rescue. Think about all you have been thru and how he was always there to help you. Do not ever hesitate to tell everyone you know about the Lord. You could save a soul!

Psalm 42:1-2
Psalm 63:1-11

Never take God for Granted

Do not look at God as if he is someone to give you what you want whenever you want it. He is a God that loves everyone but he wants you to be obedient to his Holy words and have faith in him. He is serious about forgiving sin but he wants you to be full of concern about obeying his words. God will forgive you but he does not want you to keep sinning. When you repent he wants you to really mean it from the heart. Not to keep sinning over and over again. When you continue to sin, it is as if you do not trust or love him. God is a loving God. Please take him seriously!

Psalm 70:4
Ephesians 3:18

What do you think about your Parents?

Your opinion of your parent is very important. It say a lot about you. Children should honor and respect their parents. This is to be continuing throughout their life. There are always going to be good and bad days along the way. Your parents should be someone that you can talk to anything about. I have heard people say that a parent should not be your best friend that they are to just be a parent. But I do not see it that way. Talking from experience, me and my children are like best friends. I love to tell them about the Lord. We always had a close relationship where they could talk to me about anything. We always kept the communication line open between us and that is a good sign when you can talk and encourage one another. Try hard to relate to each other with respect and love. Jesus want you to respect and love your parents. Jesus is everything that is good; a true friend. Learn to trust and obey him. He comes with peace and love!

Proverbs 22:6
Ephesians 6:4
Psalm 103:13

Grow in Grace

Thank the Lord for the patience, self- control and kindness that you have for others. If you have problems in those areas, pray to ask the Lord to remove selfishness from your heart and replace it with love for all, even your enemies. Love conquers all! It keeps you with a smile on your face. Believe that God love and care about you. God want you to enjoy life. Not sit around worrying about material things or problems at home, at school, on the job or whatever unhappiness that tries to bring you down. Spread the news about the Lord, his grace and his mercy and continue to grow in grace.

II Peter 1:2
Jude 1:2

Addicted to Drugs

If you are one that have fallen into the trap of being persuaded to use illegal drugs to try to fit in with your peers, then this message is for you. The devil can come in many forms, even drugs! He can come thru a so called friend that will persuade you to do something that is wrong. When you know down in your heart, it is not right. This friend will call you chicken and dare you to just try something just one time. Well that one time can destroy your life. This is not a friend if the person leads you to something that will get you in trouble with something that will harm you. Drugs are something that is easy to get on and hard to get off! So many teens are hooked that do not know or care which way to turn. Without Jesus in your life, you can easily get lost in sin and sink deeper and deeper toward destruction. But do not give up! God is close by you. He has never left you. Do not be ashamed to ask him to forgive you for your sins. He wants to help you more than you want to help yourself!

Psalm 38:18, 21-22
Psalm 32:3-5

When someone make a threat against you do not show fear!

Love is a powerful word. It can change things. When you are afraid, call the name of Jesus, and show love. As hard as it may sound, it works! When you are kind and humble to the enemy, they will take notice. Kindness outweighs evil every time when you have the love of God in your heart. A thug will put on a show in front of his friends, but when you get him or her by themselves, they will say that they are sorry for behaving that way. When you are covered in the blood of Jesus no fear will come into your heart when the enemy comes. Always know that God will protect you with his powerful hand. Victory belongs to him!

Luke 10:30-37
Proverbs 25: 21-22
Exodus 23:4-5

Praise is Important

Praising God is something that should be done to show God how much you love him and appreciate all the many wonderful things he has bless you with. Praising God keep you focus on who he really is. He deserves every praise to the highest! When you do good or bad on a test at school, Praise the Lord! When you win or lose a sport event, Praise the Lord! When you look back at all your many blessings, it will always show that it all came from God who made heaven and earth. Never forget who blessed you with your gifts and talents. Praise Ye The Lord!

Psalm 113:1-3
Daniel 2:20

The Keeper of the Door

Be a servant for the Lord. Dedicate your life to him. Live in a way where he can use you to help build his kingdom. A kingdom that is unmovable! Share what you know about the Lord to your peers, friends and family to save souls. Worship the Lord with Praise and gratitude. Enter his presence with thanksgiving. Feel his glory, power and experience his Holy presence as you worship him. Do not miss out on this opportunity to work for the Lord. Find time in your day for the Lord and show him how you love him and want to serve him forever!

Psalm 84:10
I Chronicle 23:5
Psalm 27:4

Believe

Always believe and know that there is nothing impossible for God. You can put your trust in him with confidence, that he is the only one that can save you! You can truly rely on him to come thru for you in so many circumstances. When all else has failed and you may not see yourself progressing, in trying to succeed at school, college, your job, or with family members. Keep the faith, never stop believing that you will achieve the good that you set out to do and that is to keep believing and knowing that God will always make a way out of no way for you! Keep your trust in the Lord that he will do what he say he will do. He does not know how to fail!

Ephesians 1: 13-14
Romans 10:11
Isaiah 28:16

Lead People to Jesus

Accepting Jesus in your life is a big step. Doing this show people that you really love him and will do all you can for Jesus in winning more souls. - That you are willing to put your life in his hands. You may think that none of your friends will want to be around you anymore. But a true friend, as soon as they see how you handle everyday problems with no stress. They will become curious to see what it is that keep you happy when things are not going well. Do not let fear make you ashamed to tell everyone about Jesus, and how he died on the cross for everyone's sin and how he arose from the grave on the third day with all power in his hands. Tell them that the victory has already been won because Jesus lives!

I Corinthians 15: 3-8
Hosea 6:2-3

Misbehaving in School

When things happen at school, like getting in trouble about something, be honest with your parents. Never be afraid to tell the honest truth of what really happened! You are to learn from your mistakes. It will make you a stronger person as you go thru life. Do not be afraid to go to Jesus in prayer. Go to him about everything! He already knows about all the pain you are going thru. Seek him with a righteous heart. He has nothing but love for you!

Zechariah 8:16
Psalm 37:37

Revenge is not yours

You know, when someone has done you wrong and you become very angry; you are to forgive them! Yes it is a hurting thing to be hurt, but think about what would Jesus do and how he would handle it! Never get angry enough to get a weapon or plot how you want to hurt someone! Do not let anger overtake you where you find yourself in trouble! Have faith in Jesus and know that his words are the real deal. He is the one that says revenge is his, and that he will take care of it, not you!

Proverbs 24:29
Proverbs 20:22

Selfishness

Sharing and caring goes along way with love. It is all about loving one another. It is so easy to be kind and show love for your fellowman. Jesus taught that we are to help the poor, needy and widowers. If you are about me, me, me, and mine, mine, mine on things you have accumulated. Remember, everything you have belongs to the Lord. We are to help the needy, not ignore them. God will bless you when you help others that are in trouble!

I John 2:15
Luke 6: 32-34
Hebrews 13:16

Working pays off better than stealing

People that go out to get a job are people that want to make an honest living. When you break into people homes and steal their valuables, you are performing evil and committing a crime! Stop trying to look for the easy way out! Stealing will damage your mind and your life. If you are hanging around anyone that loves to steal, introduce them to Jesus! Tell them how he is a healer and that he loves everyone. How he will save anyone that ask for help. When you work hard for things, for you and your family, it make you appreciate it more. When you do illegal things to increase your money; you will end up in jail! Use your mind and hands for doing a decent day of hard work for the Lord, your family and others. Be blessed by Jesus for helping the poor and people in need. Learn to love the Lord, not things!

Exodus 20:15
Deuteronomy 5: 19-21

God is Alive

God has never left you. He is with you each and every day of your life. He is there with you and sees everything that you are doing. What make him so unique to me is that he hears us, he knows what we are thinking, and he loves us and will NEVER leave us. Get to know him. Seek a close relationship with him. He is the one that is making sure no harm comes to you on your daily journey. The enemy does not want you to believe in him. When you do not believe in him and you go out on your own in this world, the enemy will try hard to attack you and your family. Satan will try hard to get you to destroy your life when you do not have God in your life. Acknowledge God, seek to know him and love him. Go to him in prayer and talk to him. He has a never ending love for you!

II John 1:3-4
Psalm 86:8-10
Revelation 15:3-4

The Earth is the Lord

We are to help keep this earth clean. God created it and put people here on earth to help make sure it stay clean and livable. The earth was not made to litter by throwing trash out car windows or cigarettes butts being thrown everywhere. It is to be kept clean as a healthy and safe environment so we as humans can live and breathe fresh air. Every part of this earth belongs to the Lord. Whenever you see trash where it do not belong, do not walk pass it! Think about how God want the earth to be suitable to live in, and then take the time to pick up the trash and put it where it belongs. This would be a great example to set for everyone and the world.

Psalm 24:1
Numbers 35:34
I Corinthians 10:26

Be the first to say you are sorry

When you have been wrong about something you said or done. Confess your mistake. Do not be so prideful, not to tell someone that you are sorry for what you have said or done. Being humble and kind is how Jesus says we are to be toward one another. Show more love and less hate! Anyone can make a mistake. We all learn from them! Telling someone that you are sorry can be a very hard thing to do. But think about how good you will feel when you get it off your chest! You have to forget about you and focus on Jesus! What would he do?

Ephesians 4:31-32
Genesis 50:15-21

Smiling has a positive effect

A frown with a sad face and evil look can run people away from you. When things are not going your way and you have destruction all around you, do not walk around or sit looking like you hate everybody! Put the best on the outside and smile no matter how bad things are. A smile can bring comfort to you knowing that things are going to get better. When you have that sour look on your face, it can bring negative thoughts in your mind, with feelings as if there is no hope because you are thinking and meditating on all your troubles. Seek the Lord thru it all and tell him about your situation. He is the way out of all your problems. He is the one that will put a smile on your face. Smiling shows a sign of happiness. Be a servant for the Lord and do it with a smile.

Psalm 67:1
Psalm 86:4
Proverbs 15:13
Ecclesiastes 8:15

Be a good Leader

Jesus wants you to be a good leader. If you have decided to be a servant for the Lord - Be a good one! Pray that others will follow your lead in coming to Jesus Christ to be saved. Invest in a good Bible, pray and ask God to lead you to a good Bible study group. Let your followers know that there is always work to do for the Lord. Pray for one another. Love one another. Whatever your ministry is, do it with love knowing that you are working for the Lord on a mission to save souls.

Daniel 12:3
Hebrews 13:7-8

I am the Door

Jesus is the good shepherd. He enjoys watching over you. Do you know that he know all about you? He sees what you go thru each and every day of your life! He is the door that is open to anyone that believes in him and wants to be saved. You have to come in thru Jesus to be saved. He is the one that can restore you. He has all you need to help you thru your everyday life. He is a comforter, a healer, a forgiver and a savior! He will forgive you and guide your every step if you let him. He has an everlasting love for you forever!

John 10: 7-16
Psalm 118:20
Revelation 7:17

Overcome evil with God

You know, Satan can come at you all kind of ways. Dwell on God and meditate on what God precious words tell you. Always be prepared to fight evil and the enemy with God's Holy words. His words are very powerful, strong and ready for battle. When evil thoughts come upon you and you start thinking crazy thoughts; start quoting God's Holy words. His words will back Satan up right out of your surroundings. Satan cannot stand the word of God. He does not like it when you call on the name of Jesus. Think healthy, happy thoughts; not envying, jealousy, or grudgeful thoughts. When you stay fixed on Jesus in your mind and heart. There is no room for Satan, he has to GO!

Roman 12:21
I Peter 3:9

Be Yourself

You do not have to impress anyone! You know who you are and God created you special in your own way. Your peers are nothing to impress because we are all the same in the eye sight of God. You should not change for anyone! Whenever someone get to thinking that they are better than the next person. They need to look at themselves and come down off that high horse! A person should never look down on a person with criticism. Instead of talking about the person; pray for them. No one will ever be better than the next person because God has no favorites! Be yourself and things will go well for you. Jesus did not change for anyone!

Romans 2:11
Galatians 2:6
Ephesians 6:9

Face It!

Would you believe there are teens that drop out of school with excuses like: classes are boring, I get bullied at school, the teachers are mean and they do not care. There are drugs and racism in school and I am afraid of the gangs. The list goes on and on. One thing you fail to realize is that, there are always going to be problems like these but you have to stay in school. God can handle anything that is bothering you. He does not want you to run away from it. He want you to face it! Learn how to lean and depend on Jesus. Ask the Lord to forgive you of your sins first. Be sincere with a made up mind to go to him. Go in prayer to him with all of your worries and concerns. Talk to him and name all of your enemies to him, one by one. Trust him to make a way out of no way for you. Then stand back and watch the wonders of the Lord; he will protect you!

Roman 8:37
John 6:37

The Early Bird catches the Worm

Starting out early to reach your goal is a positive thing. It will always bless you with something good. Dragging along is not a good thing because it show a do not care attitude and you can miss out on so much when you arrive at your destination late. Have you ever went to a job site for work or saw something at a store and the hiring supervisor say we hired someone for that position an hour ago or we sold the last item of something you really wanted, thirty minutes ago. It makes you think; If only I had just been here a little earlier. When you love the Lord, no one has to tell you to get up early to spend some time with him. You should want to spend some quiet time in prayer and study his Holy words. He should be the first that you seek when you wake up. Put him first in your life early in the morning and feel and know that you are covered and protected the rest of the day.

Isaiah 55:6
Psalm 145:20
Psalm 32:6

He reward those who sincerely seek him

God see, hear and know everything that you do in your everyday life. He know when someone is serious or not about him. He will reward you when you truthfully seek him. When you go out to tell your friends, family, co-workers and neighbors about God, remember, where two or three are gathered, he is there in the mist. As you tell others about him, tell others how he wants them to be honest in their search for the truth. Search with all your heart and soul. He wants to be known but you have to want to know him! You must truly believe that God exist. Have faith in Him!

Hebrew 7:19
Proverbs 3:13, 12:14
I Peter 1:9
Psalm 9:10, 119:130
Jeremiah 29:13

The Down Payment

The Holy Spirit is the love that is down inside your heart. It is God's assurance that we are his with eternal life for us. The Holy Spirit is what makes you love people. Make you want to do what is right in life. Make you happy inside and let you know that God love you. It gives you no doubt but love in knowing that we are his forever. When you do wrong, you will feel sad for what you have done The Holy Spirit is all about love for everyone. It will change you completely!

II Corinthians 1:22
Ephesians 4:30
Romans 8:23
Philippians 3:21

Life on this earth is not all there is

When you wake up in the morning, do you thank God for waking you up; or do you look at it as if, oh well, this is another day! Do you get started with your regular routine of putting yourself first or do you take time to think that each day is a day you want to do something special for the Lord? If you fix your life on world standards, like money, good reputation, power, and living like this from day to day until this world end, you will miss your blessing. We are to love God with all our heart and soul, and to love others, to be concern and caring. We are not to cherish things of this world. This world and things are going to be destroyed by fire. This is not our permanent home.

**Philippians 1:20-21
Galatians 2:20
II Peter 3:10**

Uncompromising Faith

Stay true to God. Never let anyone turn you against him! Be content with the way God has created you. Stay faithful to him; he loves you. He is very real! Tell everyone all he has done for you. Be humble with patience when others question you about your faith in Jesus. As you show your love for Jesus, pray that others will open up to draw closer to the Lord. Your friends and desires should never be put ahead of the word of God. Continue to be faithful! Accept God's word with a made up mind, to always be obedient to his Holy words. Have faith and believe that his word is to never, be compromised for anyone or anything.

Psalm 119:1-4, 10,15
Joshua 24:15
I Peter 3: 15-16

Take the Lord with you everywhere you go!

Learn to put God first in everything that you do. Before you leave your home every morning, Praise and thank God for all he has done for you and ask him to be with you all thru the day and wherever you may be. Take some special time out in your busy day to pray, study the Bible and to thank God for his love and protection! Acknowledge him, thanking him for all his many wonderful blessings. Thank him for the shield of protection and his holy angels all around you and your family. Thank and praise him every single day of your life as you walk in faith!

Psalm 31:23
Proverbs 2:8

Read It!

The Bible is a very powerful book. It is God's Holy words that came from him. His words can help you with any situation that is going on in your life. When you truly dedicate some time to study God's Holy words, your life will change for the better. During the good times in your life and during the bad times in your life God has encouraging words for you. Tell everyone you know about the Bible to read it. Do not knock it until you tried it! Unbelievers will try to steer you away from the Bible. Satan do not want you to know how powerful the Bible is and how it can keep him away from you. The Bible is like medicine to your soul. Read it! The Bible is the GOOD BOOK!

I Thessalonians 2:13
I Thessalonians 1:5

Step back from Bullying!

One of the best things a person can do in their life is to never, ever bully anyone. I was bullied when I was in the seventh grade and it is not a good feeling. Can you imagine when you are in the hallway at school or in class or outside in the courtyard or at lunch, a group of kids come around you trying to embarrass you in front of everyone! Well, that happened to me all the time. I was like a sore thumb that stood out in front of everyone. First my family had moved me and my sisters from Georgia to Illinois. I had a southern accent, a big nose. I was a cry baby, my clothes was always a size too big and on top of all of that, my name was Maryjane. My family had moved us from the country to the city. I felt like a walking target! I had very low self–esteem and I did not know how to call on the Lord back then. One day about nine girls that usually bully me, approached me in the hallway at school and told me that they were going to take up for me if anyone else say anything mean to me. They said, you are a nice person and you do not bother anyone. I said to myself, most of these girls are the ones that were bullying me! Now they are trying to be nice to me! I did not know what to say to them. I told you my experience of being bullied when I was young to tell you this: God had his angels and his arms all around me. He was keeping me safe with his protection all around me. Those girls wanted to say that they were sorry but did not know how, but to behave friendly toward me. No matter what you face in life, believe me when I tell you that God see everything. I know because he came to my rescue!

Psalm 66:16
Psalm 71:15,24

Who gives Wisdom?

God give wisdom to anyone who seeks it. A person that has love in their heart for people that is gentle, willing to put others first and love and respect God show genuine wisdom. When you have the love of God in your heart, you will not envy people, or be selfish or jealous of anyone, or gossip about anyone. The wisdom that come from God will show you how to love, be humble, kind, and always sincere. It is wise to do good instead of evil. We were taught right from wrong as a young child. It is wise to receive salvation by trusting in Christ Jesus!

Ecclesiastes 8:1
Proverbs 2:6

Work Together

If you go to church and participate in church worship and so many other church programs, you will notice how some members can get along and some that love to stir up trouble with petty things. If you cannot get it together in church, how are you going to get it together in heaven? You have to learn how to work together for God. You go to church to worship and praise God! Not to be a show to try to impress people. Learn how to forgive and love each other. To ask the Holy Spirit to come into your heart and to let peace begin with you!

Psalm 133: 1-3
Psalm 134:1-3

God Control Circumstances

God cares about you and your family and all of your friends. Did you know that!? He cares about everyone. That means that whatever problem may occur, he will repair, provide and make you stronger thru it! So there is no need to worry or be stressed about your day after day awful situations. There are many problems that come along with going to school and everyday life by itself! But whatever yours may be, give your problems to the Lord. Give all your headaches to him. Do not let it hang on you. There is nothing you can do about it but to tell the Lord about it. He can make it right!

I Peter 5:7-9
I Thessalonians 5:16

Get God's Advice

Some people when trouble comes will search everywhere for help. They look high and low and go any and everywhere trying desperately to get the help they need. This is a habit that most people have adjusted to, putting their trust in doctors, lawyers, their family, friends and even people off the street that you do not know, but not on God! The main important source is God. He will never lead you astray but aim you in the right direction. Instead of making him your last choice, make him your first! Always put your trust in him. He has power over everything. He has the answer!

Hosea 13:4
Isaiah 45:21-22
Psalm 31:14-15

I cannot find anything to do

Stop complaining about not being able to find anything to do when you are out of school or off your job and at home. There is plenty to do! You can ask to help with chores around the house. You can read your Bible, start a Bible study. You can help a neighbor by cutting their grass, washing their car. You can volunteer to go pick up grocery for the elderly. You can be a mentor to someone. You can cook a meal for the poor and needy. Young people are always saying that they are bored and cannot find anything to do. When you reach out to help others, God will bless you!

I Corinthians 13:7
II John 1: 5-6

The Meek Shall inherit the Earth

Do not take a person's kindness and humbleness for weakness. When you take time to talk to someone that is timid and meek, do not take it for weakness. It just shows that they have love in their heart for people with a Christ like spirit. When you have the right tone in your voice and not a harsh anger tone, you can get your point across better! If you have a nasty attitude with a short temper, ask the Lord to replace it with love in your heart where there was hate. He will always come thru for you, plus you will like yourself better!

Matthew 5:5
Psalm 37:11

Dealing with Step-Parents

I use to hear people say when I was growing up that life can be what you make it. I really did not understand that statement as a teenager. I always tried to be a jolly person. I had a friend that moved in with her father and step mother. The father was happy for her to stay with him but his wife was jealous of his daughter and did not like her from the start. She was mistreated and belittled very badly. I would encourage her all the time and tell her that she was loved by God. I told her to take the negative and turn it into a positive. She Prayed to the Lord and put her trust in him. She stayed humble and obedient to God. Jesus fought her battle for her. When things are going wrong for you with your step parents, do not argue back with them. Just meditate on what God's precious words say. Keep your trust and faith in him and you will definitely see a change in them and you!

Psalm 36:7
Psalm 130:5
Colossians 2:6

Be Courteous

Showing manners to people is something that should come regularly from you. Even when you approach people and some may have a bad attitude toward you, still be courteous! You do not know what is going on with a person when they are acting disrespectful. They may be sick, hungry, broke, sad or so many other terrible things that are going on in their life. Never come down to their level of rudeness! By you being humble and kind, something you say could make them think about how wrong they were toward you. Never block your blessings by being mean and selfish. Keep a happy spirit, stay close to the Lord, and meditate daily on his Holy words! He is the one that bring peace with a smile. When people see how you live and show love for others. They will want to come around you to see if they can get what you have and that is GOD!

I Peter 3:8
Roman 12:17

Be a Help to the Teacher, not a Problem

Going to school should be something you cherish and thank God for because it should be a happy experience, not something you dread! Learn how to pray before you leave home for school. Ask the Lord to walk with you to protect you all thru the day. To have his Holy angels all around you, to help you learn and be a help to the teacher without a bad attitude toward them and to be kind and loving with a heart to show love to everyone you meet, no matter how awful they may seem. When you put God in everything, you will see how he will help you thru any situation. He will be with you thru the good and the bad with you learning, making you a better person to succeed in life, and never giving up. Learn to learn in school. Do your best and be blessed!

Colossians 3:12
I Peter 4:8
Proverbs 10:12

Who Can You Help?

Have love in your heart to help anyone, especially someone in need. There are prideful people in this world that are ashamed of their situation that would never ask for help. When you see someone in need, try your best to help them! *"Whoever is generous to the poor lends to the Lord and he will repay him for his deed."* - **Proverbs 19:17 (KJV)**. Be kind, gentle and loving to people that are facing hard times. If you have been an uncaring person in the past, pray and ask Jesus to remove that uncaring spirit and he will! Think of some way to help someone in need. Do it today!

Proverbs 17:17
Proverbs 14:21
Psalm 12:5
Deuteronomy 15:4, 11

Feeling Neglected

These days and times have so many things with life that is happening in the fast lane. So many parents are wrapped up and dedicated to their jobs that require long hours at their job, where they do not spend enough time with their children. The neglect can easily lead children to other things; like hanging with the wrong crowd, drugs and getting into something or anyone to spend some time with that mean them no good. Do not go astray looking for the wrong thing to take the place of a parent or guardian. Seek Jesus, go to him in prayer. Ask him to show you the way, to strengthen you and to touch your parent or guardian's heart where they can spend some quality time with you. Never let hate come in your heart for your parents. Let love and understanding take the place of any sadness you may be feeling. Look to Jesus that has his love and his arms wide open for you!

Romans 15:4, 13
Psalm 118:24

Stop Condemning another Believer

Where is the love? No one should be so concern in trying to find fault in anyone. We are to love one another. Help one another. Anyone that take up so much of their time, watching someone to complain about something, that they do not like about the person, do not have the love of God down in their heart. God is love. When you see someone that is trying to get right with God and they still have some issues. Pray for them instead of condemning. God showed love for you. Why you cannot show love? Check yourself before you judge someone. You might be entitled to the same harsh judgment!

Romans 14:13
II Corinthians 6:3

Abandon by Father and Mother

I do not know of anyone that has ever been abandon by their parents. But I can imagine the horror of being left alone with no love one to care for you. I have read and heard about so many people that this has happen to and I would not wish this on anyone. But one good thing to know is that the Lord will never abandon you. He loves you with an everlasting love. Do not feel alone or not loved because God has a love that will never die. Tell the Lord all about your situation. He is willing to help you. Repent of all your sins, and ask God to come into your life and he will, no doubt about it! He will be your mother, your father, your sister, your brother and your friend. Do not be ashamed of him. How much do you love him? Diligently seek him!

Romans 8: 35-39
Proverbs 2:1-2

Promote Heaven's Interest on Earth

Concentrate more on heaven then of things on this earth. People seem to worry about the material things of this world that is going to waste away. It is a good thing to think about one day we will not live here on this earth anymore. That one day if you live right, you will dwell with Jesus in heaven. You will not have to worry about getting sick or growing old. You will never have to worry about bills, food or money anymore. You will never die. We are to set our heart on Jesus and seek him and not worry so much about the material things of this world. Keep the Lord in sight of your life!

Matthew 6:20-24
Matthew 20:15

God's Way to Life

No one ever said that going thru life would be a bed of roses. It comes with blessings and trouble, happiness and sadness with many stumbling blocks along the way. But thru it all, God is forever with you to comfort, guide, encourage and make provision for you. Love him and praise him for the good and bad. Praise God each day of your life. When you think about all that God has done for you. It should be easy to praise him. *"Let everything that has breath praise the Lord. Praise ye the Lord."* **- Psalm 150:6 (KJV).** God is worthy to be praise!

Colossians 3:16
I Corinthians 10:31

His Workmanship

You should always look at yourself as something great because God created you. Do not ever put yourself down or feel like you are a failure because you are not and will never be! God's workmanship is unique! You are to serve God and your fellowman with love and gentleness. Not to do it just to be doing it! But because you love and have a caring heart for everyone. You should be happy when you see people do very well in life; not envy and talk bad about them! God want everyone to advance in life. When someone does wrong, tell them in a decent way how to get back on the right road and that is with Jesus! You have to be concern, caring about them. Helping one another is what it is all about when it comes to serving the Lord. He love you and he want you to love your fellowman the same way!

Ephesians 2:10
I Peter 4:11

Have Fun in this Life

How do you look at life? Everyone is going to have their ups and downs. No one needs to sit around feeling sorry for themselves when things do not go their way. One good thing to know is that you have a God that love and only want to see you progress and have the best things in life. Some people think that going to church and spending time with the Lord can be boring. If you go to church just to go to church and do not take time to study God's Holy words, or do not take in what the preacher is preaching about, then it probably will be boring to you. Try hard to put God first in your life. You are not going to lose anything or miss out on something if you show love for God! Have a serious talk with the Lord and ask him to forgive you for all your wrong doing. (sin) Ask for understanding of his precious Holy words as you study his words. Trust in him! The more time you give to the Lord, the closer your relationship will be with him. It feels good to love him and to be obedient to him. Love life with God in your heart! When you follow God, you will find happiness. Have fun in believing and belonging to God!

Jude 1:2
II Peter 1:2

Anyone can be Forgiven

Every church in the world should be a place of healing for repentance and forgiveness. No one should be denied the opportunity to seek help from the Lord's house of worship and prayer. God love everyone and every culture. *"God has made it very plain that we are to forgive others. That when you refuse to forgive someone God will refuse to forgive you."* - **Matthew 6: 14-15**. Do not think that you are too good to forgive your fellowman. God forgave you!

Isaiah 1:16
Matthew 18:21-22

The Lord is the Strength of my Life

When you give your life to the Lord and change your life for him. Problems will come upon you to make you stop. Do not get weak and give up! Sometimes when you are in school and things may not go the way you had planned. Bad grades, being bullied, talked about, used and abused, no friends. You feel drained as if you are just there! Plus at home there is no relief there, with your parents questioning you about your grades, your attitude and so many other things. You wonder now what to do. Pick up your Bible, read God's Holy words and go to him with all of your sadness. Sometimes it may seem that your heartache is unbearable. You feel lost and do not know what to do! Start talking to the Lord. He will give you the strength to read his precious words. He is always there for you, waiting for you to come to him. Draw closer to God each and every day of your life. You will never regret it!

I Chronicles 16:11
Philippians 4:13

Discipline Must Come

When someone correct you for something and explain to you the right way about the situation, do not get upset. This is all about life. You have to be taught what is right and what is wrong even if you do not like it! This is how you stay out of trouble. This is how you learn about moral values and having respect for yourself and others. You cannot have an attitude as if you think you know everything! Because you do not! You are never too old to learn something new! God want you to be a beautiful person, inside and out. Learn to give people what you want to come back to you. I would hope that would be something good. Kind words, a smile, encouragement, unconditional love and respect. This is how the Lord say we are to care for one another and to always put others first. God demonstrated discipline with many to show his love!

Proverbs 13:24
Proverbs 23:14
Proverbs 22:15
Proverbs 19:18

You

1. You are loved.
2. You were created by God.
3. You are a child of God.
4. You have life!
5. You are out in the world.
6. You make mistakes.
7. You want to succeed in life!
8. You have feelings!
9. You want to be happy!
10. You have problems just like anyone else!
11. You have had times in your life when you did not know what to do!
12. You had to smile to keep from crying!
13. You have been talked about!
14. You were lied to by many!
15. You are tired!
16. You need to stop living in sin!
17. You need to get your life in order!
18. You need to get busy for the Lord!
19. You may not have another minute, another hour or tomorrow!
20. You need to make a choice on who are you going to serve; God or Satan!
"YOU"

Psalm 32:5, 8-9
Jeremiah 29:13

Giving

You know God is good when he bless you with blessings for you and your family. When you see where you have been blessed abundantly, do not forget about the poor and needy. There could be someone at your school that is trying to work a part time job to help their parents at home with the bills; or a student that want to play football and their parents cannot pay for their shoes; or a student that made it on the cheerleading team but cannot come up with the money for the Pom Pom's and her shoes! There are a lot of students at school with needs that they keep to themselves because of their pride. God told us to love our neighbors and our neighbor could be anyone. Be a person that cares about others first and give to people in need. It is the right thing to do!

Proverbs 14:31
Matthew 6:3-4
II Corinthians 9:7

Thy Word is a Lamp

You will see as you go thru life that the world is fill with so much evil. We live in a world where it seems as if it is getting terrible every day. Without the word of God, we would be lost not knowing what to do. But God's Holy words are a guide for our everyday living, of how to live in this world with the Lord on our side. It brings a message of reassuring that we can conquer anything, with the help of the Lord. So do not let fear into your heart but the love of God, to guide you every step of the way. He will keep you on the right path with his word!

Psalm 119:97, 101-105
Psalm 19:7

Do not let Success go to your Head

It is amazing and a great feeling when God bless you with good health, and financial blessings that come from the East, the West, the North and the South! Do not ever forget to thank him. Acknowledge that he is the one that gave you those blessings and no one else. Some people seem to never mention God when wonderful things come their way! It is not all about you. God giveth and he can take it away. So do not forget where you come from and the people that helped you along the way. Praise him in the morning! Praise him at noontime! Praise him when the sun is going down!

Psalm 30: 6-7
Ecclesiastes 2:26

The Way of Life

Take time to ask the Lord to help you along the way as you go thru life. You are going to have some days that go well for you and you are going to have days that make you sad. God did not say that life would be a bowl of cherries. If everything always went perfect for you in your life, you would not know how to handle it when things go wrong. You would never need the Lord or try to find out anything about him. Do not put God at the end of your list. He is the way thru life and the only way you will make it in this life. Do not let anything or anyone pull you away from the Lord. He is about the good life and how to love. Not evil ways and how to hate!

Deuteronomy 30:20
Amos 5:14

Say Hello to a New Day

A new day to know that we still have God by our side; this give you so much to be thankful for. He promised that he would never leave us or forsake us. A day to tell the world more and more about him! It is a blessing to live to see another day. A day that is fresh and new. God is an awesome God that loves us unconditionally. Each day you should give some time for God. This is another day to do something good with your life. Do not waste it on doing something sinful. Take it as a day to serve the Lord. Visit the nursing homes, feed the homeless, pray for the sick, donate money, and help the poor and needy people! Ask the Lord what is it that he would have you to do for him? We are to always ask the Lord for guidance. Each and every day, ask the Lord to show you the way, to help you. Stay obedient to God's word. Take every day as a day for the Lord!

Psalm 34:3
Psalm 16:7-8

A Flower

Flowers, flowers, flowers. They look good, smell good, come in all shapes and forms and can be used for sad or happy occasions. But today let us use them for a happy moment that needs to be shared. Some times when flowers are presented to a person they may think it is a gift to cover up something the person presenting it has done wrong! Not every one looks at it that way. Probably some one that hardly ever get flowers might joke and think that way! But showing love and kindness to one another is something that should be practice every day. It is a healthy thing to strengthen the immune system with a smile and laughter. When you show love and exercise a life of making someone happy, God smiles on you. A flower may be simple but it is a picker upper! You are showing the love. Whether to a classmate, a neighbor, a family member or a homeless person, go out the way to show that person that they are loved and needed. Show the love by your actions. Keep the love of God always in your heart for everyone!

Hebrews 10:24
I Thessalonians 4:9

Getting to know our Lord and Savior Jesus Christ

Set some time aside for Jesus Christ first! I know you may have a lot on your plate. School, studying, tests, home chores, going to the mall with your friends, on face book, texting and so many other things that take you away from the Lord. Welcome him into your life, and then diligently seek him with all of your heart. Study his words, the Bible. Change your way of living for the world and live for him! The same way you would put all these other things ahead of Jesus. Turn it around where Jesus is first in your life! Then as you study his words, meditate on them. It will draw you closer to him. Learn how to go to him in prayer with all of your problems. Ask Jesus to guide you as you get closer to him. He is already a jump ahead of you!

II Timothy 3:16
Romans 15:4

Stay Strong in your Faith

There may become a time, when it will get where so many people and businesses will not want you to talk about the Lord or mention the Bible anywhere! Some areas are doing that now. I tell people to read the Bible daily and learn to memorize God's word where no can take his words out of your head or your mouth. His words are the truth and will stand when everything else fail. Learn to be solid and anchored on your faith in God. Speak up, and do your all for God. Do it with an everlasting love for him!

I Corinthians 16:13
II Corinthians 1:24

Love one Another

What is so hard about loving people? Is it going to make you look bad? Will it hurt your ego? Is it not cool? Will it embarrass you? Do you think that you are too good to care about someone else? Do you love just who you know and forget about anyone else, or do you have an attitude of, I do not know those people, why should I care? Jesus said that we are to love one another! To care for the poor, widowers and needy people. To have love in our heart for everyone. It is so easy to be kind and loving to people even if you do not know them. Could you walk by watching someone get beaten to death, a child being abused, someone being robbed, a person on the street laying down in the cold with nowhere to go? A person that try to pay for their food and do not have enough money? Can you pass by those things and so many others that need help and not try to help or do anything for them? If you said yes, pray and ask God to put love in your heart and to show you the way. His way!

Romans 12:10
I John 4:11

It's Amazing

If you were to think about all that you have been thru, the good and the bad, it would definitely make you realize that Jesus was there all the time. When things were going bad for you and it seemed as if no one cared; Jesus cared. Even though you may not have known how to call on him, he came thru for you anyway. Think about all the good things that he blessed you with. Acknowledge him and always thank him for your blessings that came from him also. He is so amazing where he will help you in any situation because he loves you. Do not be ashamed to tell the world about him. Jesus said if you be ashamed of him he will be ashamed of you. Meditate on him and soak in his glory because he is so amazing!

Psalm 36:5
Psalm 57:5
Isaiah 9:6
I Chronicle 29:11

The Fruit of the Spirit

Live to have love in your heart for others. Do not envy or be jealous of anyone. Always have patience, show kindness, and self- control. When you have the Holy Spirit down inside of you, it would be very hard for anyone to make you angry. You will have a positive mind with peace and joy in your heart. Imitate Jesus and his way of caring for people. Do not be in a rush so much, as not having time for people, where you only think about yourself so much. You will find that being kind to your fellowman gives you such a remarkable feeling of love all around you that no one can ever take away. Live, being kind and loving, so God can use you!

Galatians 5:17-18
Galatians 5:22-23

I am not a Quitter!

So many people love to look for excuses to give up when things start to go wrong. They start to feel sorry for themselves and think of so many reasons not to go on. The easiest thing in the world to do, is to give up! When you give up the devil win! If it seems as if your life is falling apart, you go to the Lord in prayer about your problems that is coming from all directions. Ask him to help you and to strengthen you where you are weak. Satan will try to put all kind of crazy thoughts in your mind. Right when things start to fall apart in your life and when you are not use to heartache and pain. Satan will attack you when you are weak and vulnerable. Always stay close to the Lord and take time to read what his precious Holy words say; they are very powerful! God can restore anything. You have to learn how to believe and trust in him. With God you will never quit, just move forward!

Isaiah 63:7
Jeremiah 9:24

A Selfish Heart

In this life, there is enough love for everyone. There is no need not to show love to your peers. If you see a classmate that need a pen or pencil or paper or anything that they seem to be short of for class, do not wait to be ask; offer the product to them. It is a sad thing to be selfish with what you have and not help a friend in need. Love is what heals the soul. Show more of it! This is how Jesus says we are to love and show love for each other. Learn to be considerate and think of others more. They are to be at the head of your list always! Learn to put others FIRST!

Philippians 4:5,9
Romans 12:9

Smoking a Killer

Have you ever tried anything at school for fun just to be cool with your peers, like smoking a cigarette? Well, I tried it once when I was in the seventh grade. Me and my friends lit one up in the restroom and passed it around so each of us could get a puff. I almost cough my lungs out, plus the taste was awful. I knew right then that I would never try a cigarette again. It is an unhealthy habit. God's Holy words say that we are to take care of our body. Trying to fit in by doing something that could be habit forming and ruin your life is very dangerous. Pray to God to help you resist all temptations! Fit in by telling people about God and serve him, not Satan!

Matthew 26:41
Luke 22:40,46

Be Still and Know that I am God

Each day take some special time to slow down and give God the praise that he is worthy of. Think about all that you have been thru and how he came thru for you as you praise him all thru the day. Be committed to him by thanking him as you spend some quiet time with him! You have so much to thank him for; your life, your home, family, friends, and your school. Your job, your health, your financial blessings and so much more! What would you do if you did not have him? You would be at a standstill, not getting anywhere!

Psalm 46:10
Psalm 48:1

God the Creator

God is about love. He created everything and loves everyone. He created each and every one with special talents so we can help one another. He gives everyone a chance to make up their mind if they want to trust him and put their faith in him or not! The worst mistake you could make is to delay reading the Bible. Do not miss out on living eternity with our Lord and Savior Jesus Christ. Do some serious searching on his words. See for yourself how kind and awesome he is. God created the world and you are here because God created you! For you did not create yourself!

Psalm 100:3
Colossians 1: 16:17

Never Take Matters in your own Hand

Some people in this life, one time or another, has come across someone that has ruffled their feathers. Keeping calm can be a problem sometimes. Trying to deal with a bad situation on your own is not a good thing to do. Jesus wants you to tell him about it and he will handle it for you. He is all about love, not sinful things. He tells us not to worry about the terrible things that come our way. Just tell him! Put your faith and trust in Jesus today and always. Victory comes from him, not you!

Psalm 37:8-9
Psalm 75:2

The Foundation of Salvation

As you grow in Christ and get closer to him. You will find that the living word is Jesus Christ. The Bible is the written word that can feed you as you hunger for the word of God. As you study the word of God, it will make you want for more! Christ is the Fountain of Salvation. Repent of your sins. Put your trust in Christ. Seek a personal relationship with God and live for him. The Bible is your daily bread where you can be fed 24-7!

Luke 3:8
John 15:6-7

You Tried Wrong, Now Try Doing Right!

Some people have experience the feeling of getting in trouble; they know how it feel. Have you ever thought about the situation and what you could have done differently? When you see that you are not moving forward to something good and you continue to stay in a rut of failing, it is time to make a change in your life. No one wants to be a failure. When you ask God to forgive you for your sins, He will forgive you and never bring them up again!

James 4:17
I John 1:9

Run and Not go Weary

If you are living right, by loving God, by doing good in school, by loving your neighbor, by being obedient to your parents, by being kind and humble to your enemy, by caring for the poor and needy people, then you are going in the right direction of how God say we are to live and love everybody. Continue to live a good and happy life by spreading and sharing your love to others. Stay strong in your walk with the Lord by being obedient to his Holy words and never give up on him! He has nothing but love for you!

Galatians 6:9
Isaiah 40:31

Me, Me, and My, My, Mine!

Everything that you have, house, car, clothes, money, food, land, children, mother, father, dog, cat, or whatever you have, came from and belong to the Lord. There are so many people in this world believe that what they have, they made it happen. You cannot make it in this world without the Lord. Why is it so hard for some people to acknowledge the Lord? He is the one that has blessed you with everything that you claim is yours! So stop saying, this is mine and that is mine or thinking that it is all about you! As long as things are going great in your life; you have good health, a good job and a great family. The best children, money in the bank, beautiful friends, a lovely home, a nice car, nice neighbors and everything seem to be going fine. Some will never acknowledge the Lord or seek him! Some look at it, as if he does not exist and they do not know him, or will ever try to know him! But let sorrow and pain step in to try to bring you down. It can wear on you so bad, where you will run to the Lord as your last option! Do not live your life without God in it! Acknowledge him. It is all about him! He is the one that is in control; not man, or you!

Psalm 12:3
I Corinthians 1:31
Galatians 6:14

Depressed

Depression will weigh you down with worries and sadness that can bring harm to your mind and body. The best doctor I know for depression is Jesus! Remember that he is the one to rush to when you are sad and lonely. When you go to him with your troubles and dwell on what his precious words say how he will handle it for you. There will be no need to worry! Stay focus on how mighty and powerful God is and how he is always ready to help you. When he tell you not to worry! He means it! Never doubt him. He is the reviver!

Psalm 42:5-6
Lamentations 3:24

A Foreigner

We all need directions. Every day you are to seek God's guidance as you travel thru life. While you are here on this earth, you should want to live right, to be obedient to God. With his help, he will put you on the right path as how you should live. If you ask, he will show you your purpose for being here on earth. You need some loving directions because without it you could follow the road of destruction, with stumbling blocks and problems as you step out on your own. This journey is hard without the Lord. If you trust him, and follow his Holy words, he will lead you with his angel's right beside you, every step of the way. He is the one that can make it better for you and show you a peaceful way of living in this world. Seriously seek him to find your way. Do not miss out on the purpose you are here for!

Psalm 119:19
I Chronicles 29:15
Hebrew 11:13

Come to Jesus

Stop worrying. Stop Gossiping. Stop trying to handle everything yourself! Are you going forward or continuing moving backward? Are you tired of living like this? Why not try Jesus! He is a healer, a doctor, a lawyer, a mother, a father and a friend. He loves you and he will forgive you. No matter what it is that you have done. All you have to do is repent. That is, to ask him to forgive you for all your sins and ask him to come into your life. He already knows all about you. He is waiting for you to humble yourself and welcome him into your life. Experience the Salvation in Christ Jesus! Do not hesitate a second or a minute. Go to him now!

Matthew 11: 28-30
Revelation 22:17

When Someone Hurt Your Feelings, forgive them!

Do not ever think that you are better than the next person. Always have a forgiving heart. You can easily miss out on a blessing that the Lord have in store for you by being selfish to someone because you think it is all about you! So what! Someone embarrass you and hurt your feelings! But what about all that Jesus went thru with being lied on, abused and killed? Jesus never said a mumbling word. If you think about all that Jesus had to go thru, your feelings getting hurt is just a piece of cake! Rejoice in the Lord and be glad when someone hurt your feelings. It only shows that you are doing something right for the Lord. The enemy will always come at you when you live for the Lord. When you rejoice, Satan cannot stand it! Kindness will beat the devil every time. Forgive them! Forgive them! Forgive them!

Matthew 6; 14-15
Matthew 18:35

Cease From Anger

Going around holding grudges, finding fault in people and not having love in your heart for anyone is a sad thing. Jesus love you and he do not want you to walk around with hate in your heart for anyone. You have a lot to be happy about; you are alive! When you feel as if you do not have anything to be happy about, look around you and see how so many people are suffering that do not know the Lord. Then there may be some that do know him but will not acknowledge him. You have people in worse shape than you. Look at the people with terminal illness, some that are homeless, and some that are dying every minute from cancer. Be thankful for your many blessings and think about all the Lord has done for you and your love ones. It will surely change your attitude. Seek the Lord today, so he can teach you how to love!

Colossians 3:8
Ephesians 4:31

The Pastor and the Church

Get to know your pastor. If you belong to a church, take time to talk to your pastor. He is the one that can help you with questions you may have about the Bible. If you do not go to church, pray and ask God to direct you to the right church. The church has to be about God. Some people want to be seen and heard and do not believe in God. They say what they know people want to hear, not fearing God at all. Always see if the pastor is going by what God's Holy words say in the Bible. Nothing in the Bible should be changed to how man wants it to be. God's words are sacred and true. The pastor should never make you feel uncomfortable. If what he is saying or how he expresses himself to make you feel uncomfortable makes you feel uncomfortable, then he is not a man of God. Do not let anyone take advantage of you and that include the pastor! Stay close to God and he will protect you along the way!

II John 1-2
III John 1-4
Proverbs 12 :22

When you get angry call on Jesus

A bad temper is something you should ask Jesus to take away from you. When you confess and ask God to forgive you. He will forgive you of all your sins. Being angry sometimes can get you in a lot of trouble. Can make you say things that you wish you had not said. When you tell Jesus about your problems, you will not be so angry and anxious with not knowing what to do. He will give you a peace of mind, to let you know that he will take care of whatever it is that is troubling you. Pray and ask him for that humble spirit!

Proverbs 15:1
James 1: 20-21

Sin will be Judge

Having what you call a good time, doing wrong with drugs, sex, bullying, breaking into people homes, stealing, and lying, when you are with your friends. Make it seem and feel like you do not have a care in the world, where you can do anything you want. Well, if you come up in a world with no guidance or knowledge of Jesus or you come from a family that taught you all about Jesus and you make the decision to not do right anyway. You will be held accountable for all of your sinful actions. You will be judged by God on judgment day. Learn to show respect for your fellowman. When you lie, cheat, steal, kill and do any evil thing to try to hurt people, it is a sin. God is about loving people and saving souls. Think hard before you step out following anyone that does not mind sinning. It is easy to go out and get into trouble whether you are saved or not. Anyone can fall into sin. Seek him now while you have a chance!

Matthew 25:46
Psalm 145:20

Do Not Be Rebellious

Some teens that set out thinking they know everything, with a mind made up to not listen to anyone is heading for all type of problems. If you are angry at yourself and you have decided to make the day miserable for everyone else, please think twice. Life is short and time should be used very wisely. Whatever is bothering you, go to the Lord in prayer and ask him to help you. There are so many teens, young people and just people in general that are having problems with so much trouble in their lives. They do not know where to turn or who to talk to. Snapping at people, with a do not care attitude and being rude is not the way to handle anything. Ask the Lord to take all of that evil out of your heart and mind. Give everything that is bothering you to him. He is very happy to help you!

Proverbs 15:5
Proverbs 1: 31-32
Psalm 23: 2-3

Great is his Faithfulness

God love us with an everlasting love. He looks for people that are living in sin. The fornicators, liars, prostitutes, wife beaters, drunkards, drug addicts, bullies, gang members, child molesters, thief's, murderers and so on. He will never turn his back on a sinner that cry out for help and ask what must I do to be saved? He is always quick to forgive and he loves the sinner. This is how we are to love one another, without fault! He knows that no one is perfect but him! He has an everlasting love and mercy for us that is greater than any sin. His faithfulness gives us confident! He pours out unfailing love to all generations. God is slow to anger!

Psalm 25:10
Lamentations 3: 22-23

Thou Favourest Me!

As you stay close to the Lord you will see that all kind of awful things will get in your way, to try to stop you, and block you from following Jesus. But stay strong in the Lord. Instead of giving up, push forward with more love, faith and trust in the Lord. As you do more and more work for the Lord, get closer with your relationship with him. Trust the Lord without a doubt that he will take care of you. Know that he is pleased with you and will protect you from your enemies. He loves you more than you love yourself!

Luke 1:28
Psalm 41:11
Proverbs 8:35

Indifferent Teachers

(I am trying to cover anything that can occur in school, colleges or any teaching facility. I do not know if any schools or colleges have any teachers that have a bad attitude with the students where they do not care but I am sure they are out there!)

I went thru an incident at my high school with several teachers that had short patience with an attitude like; "Oh well'! They would say statements like; it do not make any difference to me whether you get it or not! I already have my education! They would get frustrated when I would ask a question. This left me with a do not care attitude also where I did not want to learn. I did not know what to do. Later on in life, I found out that Jesus was the answer, to help you make it thru life. With him by your side you do not have to worry about anything! I gave up back then when I was young because I was lost. To me it felt good to just give up because my worries went with it. But I also found out that giving up pushed me farther behind on my education. Jesus do not want you to give up when people do not have time for you or want to see you succeed. Run to him as soon as the problem occurs. He wants you to seek him and always pray for the person that do you wrong. Never hate them!

Mark 11:25
I Peter 2:1

Learn Righteousness

Your peers can be very straight forward in ways where you might be tempted into doing mischievous things. Your peers come with different personalities and a high level of curiosity. The word of God teaches a lot about righteousness, meekness, peace, and love. Talk to Jesus and learn about his righteousness. You can start by going to Bible study and learn about him. Never think that you have to impress a friend or try something dangerous or witty to fit in. Jesus will take you as you are. Whether you are popular or not! You are great in his sight! Ponder his words daily. He knows all about you; now learn all you can about him!

Psalm 5:12
Psalm 84:11

Get Up!

Do you know that when you sit around doing nothing, you can miss your blessings! I have heard people say, I cannot go to college or school or look for a job because I do not have the right clothes. I cannot go to church because people look at me so weird and it make me feel uncomfortable. People always have an excuse. The devil will put all kind of ridiculous things in your mind when you try to better yourself. But I am telling you to move it! Get up! Do something with your life that is positive! Wash and press the clothes that you have and make an effort to go to church, school, college and receive the blessing that God has waiting for you. Do not waste another minute doing nothing! Ask the Lord to take you by the hand and guide you on your journey, to show you the way. So you can stand tall and strong to do what he created you to do in this life!

Proverbs 20:7
Psalm 112:2
Psalm 25:13

It Will Come

If you are looking for someone to make you love the Lord, make you read the Bible and make you follow the Lord. It is not going to happen! No one will ever MAKE you follow the Lord. When you decide to ask the Lord to forgive you for your sins, it will come when you tell the Lord that you are tired of living the way you have been in sin, with so many horrible things happening to you. It will come when you are tired of being hurt and abused. It will come when you feel as if you have nowhere else to go or anyone to turn to. It will come when you fall on your knees and cry out to the Lord for help. Believe me! When you decide to give up that sinful life and live for the Lord. You will have a made up mind and COME!

II Corinthians 7:10
Hebrew 9:28
Isaiah 25:9

Be an Honest Person

It is not good to tell a lie because it will always catch up with you! It may seem like the easy way out of a mess, but it always will come back later to haunt you. What harm will it do telling the truth? Are you afraid someone will get angry with you? What are you afraid of? People will trust you more when you tell the truth instead of a lie! Even when you have lied and decide you want to tell the truth. People will love you for being honest! Have a close relationship with the Lord. He will be there for you, to strengthen you with a clear mind, to never be afraid to tell the truth. Being honest will never cause you any stress or pain. Think about what would Jesus do and you will tell the truth every time!

Proverbs 28:6
Proverbs 12:17

Perfect Timing

Time never stop! The only time, time will ever stop for you is when you die and leave this world. We are blessed to have certain time in life for everything. Without time this world would be in an awkward position. God put everything in plain sight with perfect timing. This just gives you something else to thank the Lord for; something that most people take for granted. Take time everyday in your life to give praises to our Lord and Savior Jesus Christ that love us. Take a certain period of the day to think about how awesome God is and reminiscence on how good he has been to you. Worship him, and thank him and draw closer to him each day of your life, serving him!

Ecclesiastes 3:1-8
Ecclesiastes 8:6

God's Inheritance

You are God's children and he has saved you with his blood when he died on the cross. He has forgiven all of your sins. Continue to pray for your neighbors who could be anyone. Be obedient to God. Get to know him more! Pray to receive the Holy Spirit, which will give you, patience, love and joy. The Holy Spirit is the proof of how serious you are with your faith in God. It shows that you belong to God with confidence to live eternally with him.

Hebrews 9:15
Luke 11:13
Psalm 61:5

Foul Language

Getting angry is nothing new, but you have to know how to handle it. Cursing do not make you look good or give you power! It makes you look very disrespectful! No one can ever say that they have never gotten angry in their lifetime. When you have changed your life to live for God, you are to forgive people who have lied against you. Be like Jesus, be a forgiver. Telling lies about people that you know is not true, and cursing them with bitterness toward them should never enter your heart or mind if you are to be like Christ! The Holy Spirit has power to give you self-control. It keeps you mindful of God's love. Pray and ask God to forgive you and to put love in your heart for everyone. Have nothing but good things to say to people even when someone talks to you with a bad attitude. Pray for that humbleness! Seek to be obedient to God's Holy words!

James 3:6
Matthew 15: 18-19

Contentment

Learn to be thankful for what you have. When you think about it, you really will appreciate what God has blessed you with instead of complaining. When you look around and see so many people in the world that is in need of things that you already have, it will make you very thankful. Do not be envious of what other people have. Concentrate on God and not things! The contentment in your heart should be of knowing that you have God in your life and that he is all that you need. He is a comforter, a healer, a provider, a savior. He brings peace and love. So be contented just to know him. He is a life saver!

I Timothy 6:6
Philippians 4:12

Beyond the Clouds

Are you pleased with your life? Are you saved? Do you have Jesus Christ in your life? Do you love God with all your heart and soul? Do you love the poor, needy, and widowers? Do you love your enemies? If you die today or tomorrow, where do you think you will go? Do you believe that Jesus Christ died on the cross and he arose on the third day with all power in his hands? Do you love money more than God? When you are obedient to the Lord with love in your heart for God and your fellowman, you will not have fear in your heart when Jesus come back to earth for his people. For on that day when he comes back on the clouds, unbelievers will be afraid and very sad. Live your life loving God and ready to help anyone in need. We are not to be selfish by hating one another! Be ready when Jesus returns to rejoice and live with him for evermore!

I Thessalonians 4:17
Matthew 24:30
Matthew 26:64

Show your Appreciation

When a friend or love one has gone out of the way to help you with a bad situation; thank God and show your love. When a person is down and struggling with all kind of problems, they try hard to find someone to help them. Then when they receive the help, they never acknowledge that it was God that came thru for them with all the help that they needed. Give God the praise for all your blessings. He is the one that is always right on time to help you in your time of need, God!

I Thessalonians 5:18
Isaiah 12:4

The Good land that God has given to us

God has blessed us with beautiful land, that provide us with flowing streams, fresh springs in the hills and valleys, with coconut, apple, fig, pears, peaches and banana trees that richly provide food for everyone. This is just a sample of what God has graciously given to us all thru the land. Praise the Lord and thank him every day for showing how much he loves you. Get together with friends and family to keep it clean and not pollute it with trash build up. Everyone has a job to do in keeping this earth clean. If you take care of it, you will be richly blessed, with what God promised us all and that is land flowing with milk and honey!

Deuteronomy 8:10
Deuteronomy 6:11-12

Eating Disorder

Are there times when you are heavy burden with so much on your mind, and you find yourself thinking that you can eat all your problems away? Some people use food as a comfort zone, or when they are nervous or all worried up! As long as their jaw is moving and the food is going down, they feel contented! But what about when the hurt is still there after all you have eaten! The food is working on your mind as a relief, in place of smoking, drinking alcohol, and so many other things that you do not do. Then before you know it, you have an eating disorder that will put you in bad health. You are stuffing yourself with a lot of food that will make you miserable and uncomfortable. Why not give your situation to the Lord? Ask the Lord to help you! He will give you the love that you yearn for and the help that you need. Jesus is a true loving and kind friend!

Proverbs 18:24
Isaiah 65:24

Material things will not get you to heaven!

Do not be so attached to things that are going to waste away. People love the material things of this world so much that they forget about God. They got to spend their money! Thinking more of themselves than others, they buy hair weave, new clothes, and new shoes, where they stack up on things and never think about poor people that are in need also. God want you to have the best but not over do it! Concentrate on God and what you can do for him! You cannot take things with you when you leave this world. Those things are going to get raggedy and waste away. Everything you own is going to waste away! Thank the Lord for blessing you with what you have and concentrate more on him and less on the material things of this world. Look out for the poor all over this world that are in need for help from people that do have and do not know what to do with their blessings. God bless you where you will be a blessing to someone else! Be happy to bless others first!

Ephesians 5:5
Colossians 3:5-6

What are you learning in school?

Going to school should be a happy time! About learning! History, Social Studies, English, Math, Science, Biology, foreign languages, Art, Music class, Field trips, friends, teachers, Gym, the library. So many interesting great things to learn! School is not about wasting your time bullying, talking about people, getting on drugs, or a gang, planning a fight, sex or who wore this or that! It is about getting as much education as you can and helping one another. You get to meet people that you will know for the rest of your life. Thank God every day that you have a place call school where you can learn! Do not be persuaded to do bad things in school that will steer you away from learning. If you just happen to run into anyone that come to school not to learn. Tell them about Jesus and how he only wants the best for everyone everywhere! That no matter how bad a person is struggling with their awful situation. He will always be there to help anyone that call on him. Seek to follow Jesus. He wants you to succeed in life! Take school seriously and be glad just knowing that Jesus is there with you. He can brighten any day!

Psalm 112:1
Psalm 119:16
Psalm 50:23

Slow to Anger

One of the best thing you can do when someone start up an argument is to stay calm. When you do not have much to say, the conversation will die down. Do not let the enemy pull you into the argument. Keep in mind how God want you to show love instead of hate! When you have the love of God inside of you, it will humble you. Pray for the individual that is arguing. Share with the person about how God say to be caring toward one another and how he wants us to love each other. Remember to have patience with one another. A kind word wins every time!

James 1:19
Proverbs 15:18
Ecclesiastes 10:4

Your Word

A person's word should be their bond. No one like a liar! When you tell someone that you are going to do this or that for them, be a person of your word. Do not tell them anything to just get them out of your face! If you will not be able to do whatever it was that you told them you would do, then tell them! You do not have to be afraid to talk to people. Be a truthful person. Being honest will take you a long way in life. Show love and concern for one another. You are setting a good example to express how you want to honor the Lord. Learn to stay focus on the Lord and how he would handle it. Make sure you always make time for the Lord, to study his Holy words and to keep your mind on healthy Godly things that will bring you closer to him!

I Thessalonians 5:23
Philippians 4:8
Proverbs 15:26

The Bible is like Medicine

When you study the word of the Lord, it is like medicine to your body because the Bible is about God and his son Jesus Christ. Nothing but good comes from it. It is very powerful. The Bible teaches you how to love and be happy with people. How not to find fault! How to be an encourager to people that are down and have given up on themselves. You could say the right words to someone that could save a life. The Bible shows you how to be a positive person enthused to help anyone that is struggling. It shows how to be patient and kind, how not to be jealous or rude and how not to give up and lose faith but to stay strong. It is healthy for the soul. It makes it very clear how to keep God in your life and how to always have love in your heart for mankind. Lean on God's love and forget about being so hateful! You know, hate will eventually destroy you! Keep away from it!

II Timothy 3:17
Ephesians 4:2

The Good Book!

There have been many books written, but there is only one Bible - the best book ever written of himself (God) to man; A book with scriptures trustworthy from God. It is a guide that should be read daily, that set the path of how we should live and how we can be saved. The Bible is a guide for living a pure life. It demonstrates how God want us to live for him. It teaches us what is true and what is not right in your life. It show us when we are wrong and show us how to get it right, and how to be forgiving to one another and how to love each other. It is a book that protects us from false teaching. The Bible is a powerful book with words for healing, comfort, love and a peace of mind! It is about God and his son Jesus. Listen to what God's Holy words say. His words can save your life!

Hebrews 4:12
II Peter 1:20-21

Instead of bullying someone, become their friend!

Sometime trying to keep up with the crowd will get you into trouble! Do you want friends and want to belong and fit in so bad that you would do anything! Stop trying to fit in and just be yourself! Do you like making people feel miserable? You think it's cool to have people frighten of you!? Have you ever thought what if the shoe was on the other foot!? How would you like it if someone stood around all day hounding and making fun of you!? Where is the love that I know you have down inside of your heart for people? Show the real you! Show the love that you were born with and the goodness in your heart that you have for people! Do not let Satan ruin your life with hate, by being a mean inconsiderate bully! Show love and kindness to people. Get to know them! Learn how to care about people and not be annoying and so ignorant and hateful to them! The people you are trying to impress, that you call your friends, do not care about you. If you were to get into trouble today and go to jail, you would not be able to find your friends. They would laugh and talk about you and turn their back on you. Turn to the Lord and ask him to forgive you. He loves you no matter what you have done. Think about it! The one that you waste so much time bullying could become the best friend you ever had! Stop bullying your FRIEND!

Romans 2: 4-10
Psalm 62:11-12

260

Be Strong and Courageous

Do not be afraid to talk to your peers about God. He is an awesome God. When you think back on all that the Lord has done for you, be not afraid to tell others about him. The Lord wants strong warriors who can stand up against the wiles of the devil. When your enemies are all around you, stay strong in the Lord. Hold your head up, feel safe and secure never doubting him. Never be afraid to tell anyone about the Lord! *"For God hath not given us the spirit of fear; but of power and of love, and of a sound mind."* **II Timothy 1:7.** Always feel secure and loved by the Lord, believing that he will fight your battle for you!

Deuteronomy 20:1
Psalm 31: 23-24

The Lord will give you Strength

Each day should be a special day for you. Have you ever heard anyone say, Oh I forgot! Today is Monday! It is going to be an awful day for me because it is the beginning of the week. They continue with; Mondays are bad for me. Do not waste a day thinking that things are not going to go right. Every day is a great day because God is in it! Can you imagine what each day would be like if you did not have God! Satan is watching and waiting for you to get tired and just give up, so he can attack you. He wants to see you fail! He wants to see you frustrated and unhappy. He want you to never accomplish anything! But here come God! He has everything that you need. He gives us what we need to face each day with love and confidence. He gives us, strength, love, peace, and him!

Psalm 29:11
Isaiah 40:29-30

Anyone who call on the name of the Lord shall be saved

No one has to be perfect to ask the Lord for help. He wants the trouble maker, child molester, lesbian, prostitute, liar, and adulterer. He will take you as you are. So many have traveled down the wrong road or should I say have made terrible choices in their lives that led to destruction and pain. We all have made mistakes in life and need a savior. Jesus died on the cross so that we all may live. Acknowledge your sin and ask God for forgiveness. He will not turn you down!

Acts 2:38
Acts 16:31

A Healthy Mind

God want you to have a peace of mind, not all worried up! Even though you have done so many wrong things in your life, he will forgive you of your sins. God say you can repent and turn to him. Stand strong on your faith in him. Trust him! As you live for the Lord, Satan will attack you to try to weaken your spirit. Do not let that stop you from telling your friends and family how God has helped you all thru your life. Get stronger with your faith in the Lord by reading his words daily, without any fear in your heart but love! Meditate on the Lord. Keep moving forward without stress and worries, but with God. You will see that your good days will always out number your bad days when you keep God in your life!

John 14:27
John 16:33

Let someone else Praise you

Do you know that boasting about yourself is a sin? In the Bible, it says that if you want to boast about someone, boast about the Lord! It is okay for someone else to say great things about you and for you to think enough of the Lord to acknowledge him. All of your blessings come from the Lord. Do not be stuck on yourself and just brag and boast about all what you have accomplished in life! The Lord is the one to give praise to because this is where all your blessings come from. Learn how to be thankful for the Lord and talk more about him and not all about you!

Proverbs 27:1-2
II Corinthians 10:18

God's Loving Kindness

The love of God will keep you with a sound mind, knowing that he love you and only want the best for you. God is always waiting to over flow you with his love that he want you to have so much! When everything is falling down all around you and it may seem like there is no hope or help from anyone in your family or from a friend. Do not feel sad or lowly. Always remember what God words say about his loving kindness! His words will never fade or go away. Memorize them in your mind and permanently keep them on your heart so they can stay with you forever!

Psalm 25:6
Psalm 103:17

The Fruit of his Work

There are going to be ups and downs in this life. We are to rejoice in the Lord doing the good and bad times. Be happy just knowing that Jesus is always with you. *"Rejoice in the Lord always and again I say rejoice."* - **Philippians 4:4** Love God with all of your heart. Show love, kindness and patience to your fellowman. This is the fruit of the Holy Spirit that is from Christ Jesus that lives inside of you. If you love Jesus you will imitate him. Keep love in your heart for everyone!

Galatians 5:22-23
John 15:4

New Dimensions for your Faith and Love

Stand grounded in your faith and love for the Lord. Do not ever let anything separate you from the love that you have for the lord. Trials and tribulations will come upon everyone in this life. But never forget how much God love you and will help you in time of need. You do not have to be afraid when trouble comes because his love is everlasting. Always show your love for God and other people. Keep God first in your life!

Psalm 107:8-9
I John 5:3
Matthew 22:39

How Priceless is your unfailing Love

You know, God is such an awesome God that he is willing to help anyone at any time. He has an amazing and never ending love for everyone in this world. There is no specific person, no favorites! He truly has a solid, anchored, love for everyone and will always do his best for anyone! He will never stop loving you and throw you away or let you down. Stay in contact with Jesus. Spend some long quiet hours with him to just thank him and glorify him. Show your love to him. He has a never ending love for you. He really does!

Jeremiah 31:3
I King 8:23
Psalm 100:5

The Lord is my Light

The way we live should show our love for the Lord. When others see that you are happy, even doing bad times. They will wonder and ask what is it that keeps you with a smile on your face, when trouble is all around you! This is when you can jump right in and tell them, about a man name Jesus. How he is always there when you need him. That he is a comforter, a healer, a way maker, a friend, your everything. We should be obedient daily to his Holy words and guidance, so we can let him lead the way. His way is the right way!

Matthew 5:16
John 8:12
John 1:5

Jesus in School

There is no stopping Jesus. He is everywhere. The authorities are wasting time trying to keep him out of school. He is everywhere you go. If you keep Jesus in your heart and mind and meditate daily on his precious words, it does not matter where you are! Quoting God's powerful words will make it hard for Satan to get near you. Jesus name has power in it also! Call his name whenever you are afraid; especially in school. There has been so much sadness in schools and colleges after prayer was no longer allowed on or in the premises. When you keep his mighty words inside of you, no one can touch it or stop it! Stay strong in your faith for him!

Hebrews 11:6
Ephesians 6:16-17

God Hear the Prayer of the Righteous

Repenting is important and a very serious thing when you ask the Lord to forgive you for your sins. God know when you are sincere and when you are not. Changing your life to live for the Lord is saying that you forgive your enemies. You love everyone, and you love God with all of your heart. You will have love in your heart for the poor, needy and widowers. It is a serious thing to say you love the Lord and have hate in your heart for your fellowman. Pray to God for meekness, humbleness and kindness also. Search your heart entirely and be sincere when you repent. Pray that God will strengthen you where you are weak!

Proverbs 15:29
Psalm 145:18-19

You can begin again

With God there is always another chance to get your life right. When you mess up and believe me, people will mess up but God is always there to pick you up when you are down! He wants you to come to him in prayer, repent of your sins and to tell him everything. He wants you to know that he loves you and that he is a forgiving God. Never be afraid to open up to the Lord. When you get close to him with your love in prayer, Bible study and continue to seek him. He will get closer to you, guiding your every foot step. Do not ever hesitate to show him how much you love him. It is never too late to start life anew with God!

Hebrews 9:14
I John 1:7

Green Meadows

Nature shows the beauty of how much God truly love us. It shows a lot of how he provides for us. Truly more than we need or could have ever imagine. This supply of generosity is something to be very appreciative, for it show that all of our help come from him. Food, clothes, our home and everything that we have or could ever dream of is his alone. Pray to never be selfish but generous to others.

Psalm 65: 12
Job 38: 26-27

Sexually Transmitted Diseases

This is a serious matter that all teens need to always keep in mind, especially sexually active teens. There are so many diseases out there that can destroy your life. Your body is the temple of God that is to be taken care of in a respectful and decent way. God want you to care enough for yourself that you let no one take advantage of you in any way. Learn to love yourself where you will want to care about yourself! You do not have to prove anything to any of your peers. Some people do not know this but God see everything that you do! These are not words just being spoken or made up! He watches every move you make. God want you to be obedient to his words where you will prosper and not head yourself to destruction! A sexually transmitted disease can haunt you for the rest of your life. Herpes is no joke!

I Corinthians 3:16-17
Romans 13:12-13

God did not make Wimps

Work toward a close relationship with the Lord. Get to know him. Tell others about him. Stand up for Jesus! As you get stronger in your faith for the Lord, all kind of things will try to get in your way to stop you. But let the obstacles make you stronger not weak. God needs warriors to fight the enemy which is Satan. He is not working to just interfere to slow you down from working for the Lord. He come to try to destroy you, to take you out! Do not be afraid. Meditate on what God Holy words say; *"I will never leave you or forsake you."* **- Hebrew 13:5 (KJV)** His words are the truth! He will always be there for you. Keep trusting in the Lord who will always have your back!

Psalm 118:6
Deuteronomy 31:8
Joshua 1:9

Pray Always

I know you probably want to know how do you always pray! Every day of your life is going to require some type of prayer. You can pray for others that are in need for a healing, for a financial blessing or for any bad or good situation that they may have. You can say a quiet pray as you work, at school, at the mall, during a test, or at a restaurant. There is always time to pray. It does not have to be a long prayer; something brief but sincere. As you go thru life, be concern and caring about anyone that have a problem and take the time to pray for them. Your prayers will add a blessing to them as well as you!

Ephesians 6:18
Luke 11:1-4

Do not love money more than God

Loving money, and the temporary things you can buy with money, and dwelling on how to make more money, should not be your main interest. God should be the first thing on your mind every day! If you make material things more important to you than God, then it will get to where material things and money will control you! Are you giving more time to things and money than God? Why put so much in collecting money for material things that are going to waste away. God blessed you with money to bless people that do not have and is in desperately need for help! Be caring for people and concern more for the one that do not have and GIVE!

I Timothy 6:17-19
Luke 12:20-21
Psalm 39:6-7

Be not afraid of the terrors around you

The same way God protect you in the day, he will protect you at night! With so much happening in the world, with devastating crimes that put so much fear in people, the Lord wants you to know that if you let him be your shelter, your protector and put your faith and trust in him and be obedient to his Holy words, that he will keep you safe, wherever you are in this world. When the enemy is all around you, never let fear enter your heart or your mind. Concentrate on what God say he will do for you. Feel safe and loved knowing that you are covered with his protection no matter where you are. He has his Holy angels all around you to intervene when anything evil try to come your way. Keep your faith in God with a strong mind and you will never be fearful of anything!

Job 5:19-24
Psalm 23:4

Do not tell a lie on anyone

The Bible condemns lying. It is a very serious thing when you tell a lie on someone. It can really damage a person's character, their reputation, their whole life! When you do not know anything about certain things that are going on with a person, tell the truth. Do not make things up! If you have hate in your heart for someone and you hate that person enough to lie and spread rumors about them. Then it is time for you to check yourself! Sit down and have a talk with God and ask him to forgive you and to help you! If you are angry and hate yourself, your life style! Stop it right now! There is some good in you! God made you and he has only good things for you to do for him. All the evil that come from your heart is from Satan and he only want the worst for you! Be a servant for the Lord. Change your life to do only good and decent things for the Lord and live a happy life. Do not tell a lie because it will always come back to harm you later. Do not ever let anyone talk you in to telling a lie on someone! God has good things in store for you and lying is not one of them!

John 8:44
Revelation 21:8
Ephesians 5:4
Exodus 20:16
Colossians 3:10

Believers falling prey to false teachers

Take time to study the Bible for yourself! When you take time to read the Bible, I pray that the more you read and meditate on God's Holy words, the more you will want to get closer to God. As you get closer to God, pray for the understanding of his words. Do not let anyone trick you, or try to twist what the word of God say, to what they want it to say. Not one word of God is to be change. When you research anything in the Bible, that someone tell you. Remember that what God Holy words tell you in the Bible is the truth. We all are to honor and be obedient to God's Holy word. Do not let anyone lead you wrong with what God's Holy words tell you. The truth will definitely set you free.

Jude 24
Romans 16:20

God created man to be with a woman

Man and woman was put in this world to multiply it. A world cannot be multiplied with a man married to a man or a woman married to a woman or just shacking together, which is called fornication, which is a sin also. Do not be so quick to believe lies thinking it is okay to live this type of lifestyle. I love everyone! I am not hating on you God knows I am not judging you! I just want you to know the truth and I want you to make it to heaven. God Holy words are not just something to read. It is an important message to the world of how we are to live and love one another. Anything can look good and feel good to someone that is living wrong because they want to try to make the wrong look right in their sight and forget about what anyone think about them. They block out the truth and concentrate on their desires and wants! But God Holy words will last forever and he is not going anywhere! The truth is the truth, and there is no way around it! If you really want help! If you really want to understand what God Holy words mean! Repent of your sins, save your soul and live for God. Satan wants you to go astray living in sin where you will miss heaven and go straight to hell! God want you to know the truth and to live by it!

Genesis 2:18, 23,24
Leviticus 20:13
Leviticus 18:22
Matthew 19:4-6
Genesis 1:28
282

Jesus Loves Me

God is so awesome! He has a son name Jesus that love you with all your faults. He loved you before you even loved yourself. He shows his love everyday with the hedge of protection over your family, your friends, and the entire nation! You would be lost without him. Everyone should know about Jesus Christ! No one should miss out on living for him. He will forgive you for any sin that you have done. He will not throw it back up in your face. He will not talk about you behind your back! He genuinely loves you. He loves you so much that he died on the cross so that we all may live. No one in this world would have gone thru all of the pain and suffering he did for us all! He did not just talk about his love, he showed it. Start today by telling others about Jesus Christ. Be committed to him by serving him, praising him, and studying his Holy words, the Bible. Pray to be guided to a good Bible study group. Learn about Jesus; show your love for him. Be the best you can be for him and show your love for someone!

John 15:10
Zephaniah 3:17
John 15:13

Devote your life to what really count

Give your all to working for the Lord. Tell people about God and his son Jesus who died on the cross for our sins. Do not be ashamed of him. The worldly things that have such a strong impact on young people like rap music, violent movies, and the use of computers are just some of the things that people spend so much time with, that could easily lead to destruction. Seek Jesus and his way to a better life of living right. Take time to have a nice talk with your parents and share how much you want to do better in your life. Clean up behind yourself, without being told to do so. Help a neighbor, feed the homeless. Pray to always focus on what is good. Strive to be like Jesus. If you are in the word of God, stay in the word. The bible is to be read seven days a week. The more you read, the more devoted you will feel with more love in your heart for the Lord and everyone. Never put God last in your life!

Ephesians 4:23
Titus 2:14

Whoever finds me find life!

Are you ready to give Jesus Christ your life? Are you ready to change your way of living? When you find Christ and give your life to him, He will lead you in the light, if you let him where you will never go astray in darkness. The darkness is sin, which he takes away from you to show you the way to live. To find Jesus Christ is saying that you love him. You believe that he died on the cross for everyone's sin and that he arose on the third day with all power in his hands and that you welcome Jesus Christ as Lord over your life. Once you repent of your sins and put your faith in Jesus, it changes your personality, your wants and motives from the inside out. You should always desire to follow Jesus directions from his Holy words. His words are very powerful. You will never go wrong when you find and follow Jesus!

Proverbs 8: 34-35
John 17:3
Isaiah 9:1-2

My High Tower

You can depend on the Lord as your refuge. You can trust him, never doubting that he will keep you safe. He is always near and keeps a watch where he can see and hear everything. He will not let the troubles of this world get close to you if you stay close to him in prayer. Jesus shall not be moved. You will be happy, feel safe and have a peace of mind when you have Jesus in your life. He is your defense, your protection if you put all your faith in him. Get to know him. Take time to listen to him without any distractions. Tell him about all of your worries. He will renew your mind and bring peace to your heart. View your situations from God's point of view. Nothing is impossible for God. He is a tower of deliverance!

II Samuel 22:2-3
Psalm 61:3
Psalm 144:2

Gossiping

One of the worst things to get involved in during a conversation is a conversation about someone you do not like. Gossiping can cause problems! The main person that started the gossip is going around talking about you also. Learn how to have better things to do with your life instead of gossiping. You can start with no comment and it will go nowhere. But if you add your comments to it, then it will take off. Gossiping is a sin. Stay out of the conversation. Ask God to strengthen you, and to put love in your heart where there's hate. Want to stay safe!? Talk about the Lord!

Proverbs 26:20-22
Proverbs 20:19
Proverbs 25:23
Galatians 5:15

Your life filled with his joy

When you have the love of God in your heart, you should want to help anybody in need. Always be happy to help people in need; especially when their spirits are low. It is a glorious and loving thing to do when you look out for others that are less fortunate. Show the love to others that God has given to you. Never stop caring, sharing, smiling and spreading the word about Jesus Christ! He wants everyone to be content, safe and secure and to know him. You can go to him when you are burden down and feel as if no one else cares. Jesus is always a step ahead of you, and always ready to help you in your time of need. Continue to love and help others to get close to the Lord. Keep sharing the joy in your heart with everyone!

Nehemiah 8:10
Esther 9:22
Psalm 9:2

A Thousand Fall at your side

When you are covered in the blood of Jesus with his protection, the enemy cannot touch you. Stumbling blocks will be thrown in your direction to try to keep you from achieving in life. God will step in and remove them from near you to clear the path for you. The enemy will stand there looking at you, thinking; I have tried this to hurt them and this to stop their accomplishment but it is not working! That is because God will be fighting your battle for you. Just stay obedient to what God's Holy words says and that is to love your enemy and be kind to one another. Meditate daily on what God's Holy words say what he will do. The enemy will not be able to put their hands on you!

Psalm 91:7
Luke 10:19

You cannot fix what is wrong

God is the only one that can help you with your problems. Trying to fix your situation without the Lord will only lead to more problems. The Bible is a very powerful book because the words are from God. When you have a close relationship with God, he will direct you and guide you in every circumstance. When you are in the world and do not try to find out anything about God. You will run into all kind of difficulties. The Bible tells you that you are going to have good and bad days. Follow the Lord and put all of your trust and faith in him. Trying to run from your problems is just a waste of time. Run to the Lord!

Psalm 13:5
Psalm 9:14
Psalm 20:5

Never Take a Weapon to School

This is very important! Always have a mind of your own. Never let anyone talk you into doing something that you know is wrong. Taking a weapon to school is not smart at all. What is going on so bad at school, to make you want to take a weapon to school? Has someone hurt your feelings? Did some girl or boy not talk to you or do not like you? Has a teacher made you angry? Is someone bullying you? Someone embarrassed you? Life is too short to let Satan take your mind to destroy you! Life is about ups and downs and growing up! You have to take the bitter with the sweet. The Lord wants you to talk to him about whatever is going on in your life! Do you know that he has control over everything!? Every time when pain and sorrow come upon someone, they never turn to Jesus. They try everything else but Jesus! This is how so many people get in trouble, trying to solve the problem themselves. You can always call on Jesus to help you in any situation. He cannot wait to help you!

I Peter 2:17
Proverbs 24:21
Proverbs 24:8

I am not an Idiot!

Be careful of the words that you bring out of your mouth! They can be very damaging to a person. Think before you speak! No one should be called an idiot! As you live and learn, everyone in this life are going to make mistakes. Spend time learning from them. Do not look at people and think that you are all of that when someone do or say something wrong to you. When you call someone an idiot, you are saying that they are foolish and stupid! Do not ever get frustrated with your friend or fellowman and call them an idiot! God love each and every one of us with our flaws. We are to do the same and have that love for each other. Instead of talking about the person that seem to annoy you, pray for them! Learn to love and not be so anxious to find faults!

Proverbs 13:3
Proverbs 18:7
James 1:26
James 3:2
James 1:4

I Did This and I Did That!

When you are blessed with a special talent, thank the Lord for it. He is the one that blessed you with it. Do not be so boastful and prideful that you do not acknowledge God for blessing you with your talent. God made it possible for you to have and use your talent. It is good to be blessed by God with a talent that can help you and others. No one should have to tell you to give God the praise. This should come naturally if you have the love of God in your heart. So stop boasting about all what you have done. It all came from the Lord. You cannot use your talent without him. He has all blessings in his hand!

Psalm 12:3
Galatians 6:14
Ephesians 2:9
II Corinthians 10:17

Recognition

Do not worry about if you are never recognized for the good things that you do in this life. Do not try so hard trying to please people. You will never be able to please people. They will always have something to complain about and grumble. God will never criticize you. Do all that you can for him. Trust in the Lord. Obey his precious words and one day you will be rewarded by him who see and hear everything that you do. God's approval is worth more than what anyone else thinks about you. Work hard to seek the Lord. You will see that he is the right choice!

I Peter 5:6
Colossians 3:23

Trust in the Lord Forever

You can be happy and content everyday of your life because you know your redeemer lives. Think about all the times he has come thru for you. When you thought all was lost, here comes Jesus with the answer. When you were backed up against the wall he came thru so many times for you, with a ram in the bush. You can always trust in the Lord. He is the one that is fighting your battle and is with you forever. When you are having a hard time at school, on your job or at home or wherever you maybe, keep in mind that the Lord is there with you and that he is already on the case. He has never lost one yet!

Isaiah 26:4
Psalm 37:3
Deuteronomy 30:20

Citizens of Heaven

The ways you carry yourself around others say a lot about you. If you are saved and believe that Jesus died on the cross. That should keep you with a peace of mind. Jesus expressed his love for us all by dying on the cross! You know how you love the Lord and live should show it! Do you have love in your heart for everyone? Do you love people that hate you!? Are you willing to help the poor and needy? Are you obedient to God's Holy words? Do you think more of others than you do yourself? Start today by giving more time to the Lord and others. Be humble and kind and willing to give up this sinful life by putting all your faith and trust in the Lord today. Be an authorized messenger for Christ!

Philippians 3:20
Hebrews 12: 22-23

Do not be happy when harm comes to the Enemy

When you hear that something bad has happen to the person that was bullying you, that was always making your life miserable, that continued to make you feel sad every day. Do not be happy! The word of God says that when you are happy for their hardship, it will make God turn his wrath on you. Pray for that individual that God put love in their heart, where there was selfishness and hate. Have love in your heart and only wish the best for that person. God is all about love and we all should have love in our heart for one another. Be sincere and want only the best for them!

Proverbs 24:17
Obadiah 1:12-15

I Love the Lord

Anyone can say they love the Lord. But do you show him!? You can show him by being obedient to how his precious words say we are to live. You can show him by how you treat others. You can show him by forgiving people and love one another. You can show him by telling everyone how he died on the cross and arose on the third day from the grave with all power in his hands. Start today by showing how you love the Lord and be an inspirations to others so that they will give their life to the Lord and follow him. Show your love!

Psalm 116:1-2
Mark 12:30

Breath of Life

Did you ever take time to think that the breath you breathe is from God? It comes from God's spirit. Some people never take time to think about those things. Your body becomes a shell of a body when there is no life in it. God chose to create you and gave you this wonderful gift, life! *"He breathed into our nostrils the breath of life and man became a living soul."* - **Genesis 2:7 (KJV)**. The breath of life is to be taken seriously because it was given to you from God. Never think that you are just here to live until you die. You are all here for a purpose. You are to value your life. Keep your body clean and healthy; not pollute it with alcohol, chemicals, tobacco, drugs and so many other things. Live each day being grateful to God for creating you and giving you life. Learn to love yourself more. You are a precious creation. God's Holy words speak the truth!

Psalm 103:14
John 20:22

Good Surprises (Do something good for someone today)

Today, think of someone that has been feeling down in your home or church or in your neighborhood or a friend of yours that need cheering up! Think of something that you could do to brighten their day. Show love to that person by showing that you care. This is how the Lord wants us to care for one another. Take some time to listen to the person. What you do for them will surely be a blessing for you and them!

I Peter 1:22
II Peter 1:5-7

Bless the Lord at all Times

Acknowledge the Lord, for he is your savior and your redeemer. Trust him, and show your love without ceasing. Bless his Holy name. He is your provider and a shelter with a guard all around you. When you call on him, he will come. When you are on the bus, in your car, in class, at the park, or wherever life takes you, praise him! Do not let fear make you afraid to praise him. Never forget to praise the Lord. Praise him for every gift he has given you. Give him the praise, for he is worthy to be praise!

Psalm 34:1
Psalm 71:6
Ephesians 5:20

Your Impurities

As a teen, learn to trust God and pray to him. Ask him to help you find your way from destruction that could ruin your life. When you are of this world and not working toward being saved, you could easily fall into wickedness that you will see no shame in doing; like being resentful of others, arguing, hate, deception, gossip, fornication, lying, stealing and so many other terrible things. Do not become slavery to sin. Do not follow the desire of your sinful nature. Seek the Lord and ask him to forgive you of your sins and he will! Do not let a so called friend talk you out of cleaning yourself up! You might lose some friends as you change your life but Jesus will never turn you away. Choose a life with God today!

Galatians 5: 19-21
Romans 6:19
I Thessalonians 4:7
Hebrews 10:22

Keep Can't Out of Your Vocabulary

Do you know that you can do anything that you thought you could not do? Try it! If you can go a day without saying I can't do this and I can't do that, you will find out that you can. If you do not put forward an effort to do anything, you will miss out on so much. Start today by saying that you can make a difference in life. Be positive showing that you can do anything with the help of the Lord. He is the one that make it happen! Always include him in everything that you do!

Mark 9:23
Mark 11:24
Matthew 21: 21-22

Never be ashamed of where you come from

Be who you are! It can be a very uncomfortable thing when you are trying to be someone that you know you are not! Why are you ashamed of who you are and where you live? When you pretend to be something that you are not, sooner or later the real you will come out! Thank God for creating you and if you have something about you that you do not like; pray and ask God to help you. Some people have great personalities, a great smile, a kind heart. They just be themselves being content with what they have. Some have nice homes, cars and live in a beautiful neighborhood. But all of that do not make a person. Always be happy for people and never envy or be jealous. Be thankful for what you have! Remember God see everything! Just keep trusting and learn to depend on Jesus. Your blessing is on the way!

Proverbs 30:8
Psalm 22:26

Weeping May Endure For the Night

So many people live in sin and go about life without God. They step out in the world doing whatever they like, without giving a second thought about the Lord. Thank God his anger only last for a moment. When you do not have God in your life, you can easily go astray because you do not know him. He wants the very best for you. But he wants to be included in your life. He is not going to force you to live right. He sees everything and knows everything about you. But if you do not talk to him, repent and ask him to forgive you and show you the way. You will be like a sheep that walk off among the wolves ready to be destroyed by Satan who is waiting for you to make that wrong move. But God is so good; he will go to you with the (that something told me) Holy Spirit, to warn you not to do something. But most people will brush (that something told me) off to the side and go right on with their plans. Then when you mess up, God will be right there anyway, to comfort you with his peace and love. Pray to get closer to the Lord and show your love for him always!

Psalm 30:5
Psalm 118:1

Are you a Leader or a Follower?

Are you a person that loves to follow the in crowd? That love to be around people where anything goes? Where the crowd is always up to something that will lead to trouble? Are you a person that stands on doing right, with a strong mind to know what you want out of life? Some people that are easily persuaded by others to do wrong, can easily be classified as weak. Satan work with weak people because he know it is very hard to work on a strong minded person that has love in their heart for others. Do not be a follower but a leader that love to do right and to show people the way that are doing wrong. Get into the Bible and ask God to help you to understand his precious words and to guide you where you can help others to know about him!

Proverbs 12:24
Numbers 13:30
II Chronicles 29:11

I do not Get Weaker but Stronger

As you lean and trust in the Lord. You will see your faith will grow stronger as you develop a close relationship with the Lord. You will feel lively with confidence knowing that you can do all things with God who gives you the strength. If you have anyone that you know is struggling with drug abuse, being molested, talked down to, is talking about running away from home, or cannot get along with their parents; someone that is being beaten, or talking about an abortion or feel as if they cannot fit in school; someone that is talking about doing something horrible to themselves, or talking about stripping at a night club, or planning to hurt someone, or someone that is poor and need help. Please do not turn away from them! Talk to them about Jesus and how he has never lost a case. Tell them about his sacred words, the Bible that is so powerful. Tell them to fall on their knees to Jesus and tell him all about it and he will handle their problems. Stay strong in the Lord always with no excuses, forever!

Psalm 69:13
Psalm 32:7
Psalm 40:3

How to Deal with Depression

When you are a teen growing up around so many other teens, it can be very challenging. You see different attitudes, personalities and competition. If you are a person that worries about what to wear, your hair, nails and what someone think about you then there is a chance you might get depressed if you cannot keep up with the Jones. But these are tedious things because life is not suppose to be about things and trying to outdo someone. It is about being yourself and being obedient to God. To stay away from depression, worship God and learn about him. The Bible is so amazing with powerful words. Read the scriptures, pray for understanding. Tell your friends about the Lord. Listen to soothing spiritual music and pray to receive your peace. God will give you strength to face any problem!

Psalm 138:3
Isaiah 26:3

When you do not tell the Truth

Everyone knows what it is called when you do not tell the truth; it is lying. I have found out from experience that people will lie when they are afraid. Think about it! No matter what your age, you are capable of lying when you are afraid. I have learned that when you lie it is hard for people to trust you. It is always at your best interest to tell the truth. This will set you free from having a burden hanging over your head for lying. Try to live an honest life with love where people will trust you. Lying destroys trust. Imitate Jesus. He would never lie!

James 5:12
Colossians 3:9
Matthew 5:33-37

The Victory shall be Won

When God step in to help you, to defend you, he will show you that it is about him and not man. God will always win. It is good to know that when you are walking in faith with God, that you never have to fear man. Always be prepared for the enemy. The closer you get to the Lord, the more you will want to know about him. God's Holy words are the truth and very powerful. He will always do what he says. The enemy does not stand a chance. Walk in faith everyday of your life. Be happy and enjoy your life!

I Corinthians 15:57
Proverbs 21:31
Deuteronomy 20:4

Joy Comes From Christ

When you have tried everything and you find that your troubles are too hard to handle. Quickly tell Jesus about it! The Lord promise to be with anyone when trouble arises. You have to know that Jesus is always around when bad things come your way. Trials and tribulation are no joke and it can happen to anyone and when it does, you can call on Jesus. Be patient! He is the one that bring you happiness and peace and put joy in your heart. He is the one that always make things right. Look to Jesus who can fill you with a loving heart for everyone. He is the one that keep you encouraged for the world. Keep learning and depending on Jesus. He is the one that can bring love and joy in your life!

James 1:2
Proverbs 17:22
I Peter 1:6

The Sting of Alcohol (Liquor)

What make a person turn to alcohol when problems occur? There are many reasons people turn to alcohol. Here is why some teens turn to alcohol. Violence in school, poverty, illiteracy, gangs, fear of their peers, problems at home, child abuse, neglect and much more. The high is only temporary. It causes trouble, make you forgetful, stir up strife, affect others, harms the body and it is a sin! This can happen to people that do and do not have God in their life. Truly you need God beside you every step of the way, every day of your life! Trying to handle the dreadful problems that you have in your life, will never get right, if you keep God out of it! Let him in your life! His son Jesus died on the cross to save us all from sin and to show us the way. He is the way! Go to him in prayer and tell him about the awful things that are going on in your life. He is waiting on you with his arms wide open. GO TO HIM!

Isaiah 5:11, 22
Isaiah 28:7
Leviticus 5:5
Deuteronomy 21:20
Psalm 86:5
Psalm 146:5

Be Content with what you have

In this life there are going to be times where you will see people with nice homes, cars, nice clothes and so on. These are all material things that will soon fade away. God will supply all that he thinks you need. You will never go lacking when you put your trust and faith in the Lord. You do not have to be concern about the things that other people have. Some people live everyday thinking about things that they want and think that they need. Learn to be content with what you have in every situation. Do not dwell on things and wanting more and more all the time. Use that energy to think about people that do not have and how you can help them that is really in need. Trust in God and know that he is all that you will ever need!

I Timothy 6:7
Philippians 4:11

Tackle Your Problem with a Smile

God has given you life and that is something you should be very happy about even with your struggles that come with living in society. Trying to smile when things are going wrong can be hard, when you do and do not have God in your life. I have learned that if you put the best on the outside and meditate on God's word, it will put a smile on your face and love in your heart for everyone. Sometimes when you go thru awful things in life, it is as if you are being tested to see how strong your faith is. Do not get weak and give up! This will help you develop stamina and strengthen you as you move ahead thru life!

Roman 5:3-5
Numbers 6:25

You are obligated to love one another

You are a child of God. We owe everything we have to the Lord. You may not like it but we are to love one another. Why do so many people find it hard to love one another? Most people seem to want to show love when something awful happen to someone or their family member or friend. The same love you give to someone when they are in pain, is the same kind of love you need to show to others all the time! A happy kind and loving spirit keep you healthy from the inside out. God love each and every one of us with an everlasting love that will never die. Talk to the Lord about that hate you have in your heart. Pray and ask him to remove the hate and replace it with love. You have to learn how to love doing the good and the bad times for everyone. God's love will always continue to flow, it never stops!

I Corinthians 13:1-2
I John 4:7
Romans 13:8

Pick a Quiet Area

If you take time for the Lord, he will take time for you. There comes a time in your life where you have to make time for him; a time to pray, to rest your mind with peace, with God. The world is moving at a fast pace where so many people are not slowing down. They take time to go to the movies, parties, shopping, trips, sport events and so many other things that take them away from giving God some of their time. Take some time to be alone to dedicate to God. Pick a quiet, serene, divine, atmosphere where you can talk to him and where he can talk to you. I promise you, you will be so glad that you did!

Matthew 11:29
Matthew 6:6
Ecclesiastes 8:5

Backbiting

When you have a close relationship with God, you do not have to fear what people may say about you. I had a friend tell me once that she was quitting her job because people were talking about her and telling lies on her! I told her that she should not quit her job because this happen on every job. People are going to talk about you and may even tell lies. I told her that Jesus put up with all kind of lies and he never quit telling people about his father in heaven and he stayed humble with love in his heart for everyone. I told her if she quit that job, she will always quit any job that she get, if she worry about what people say or think about her! God precious words are not here just to look at; they are his daily bread for you to follow for your everyday living. Concentrate on what God thinks; not your fellowman!

Psalm 41:7
Titus 3:2
James 1:3

The Whole Tongue

The tongue is a powerful weapon that can bring peace and it can also destroy anyone. You have to be careful, with what words you bring thru your mouth. Harsh words can damage anyone for life. There are so many people in the world that have been scarred from hurtful words, where they actually believe what was said about them! It affects some people where they cannot move on in life. They dwell on the terrible words or lies that were said about them. Cruel words that can easily pull their spirit down! Learn to control your tongue with kind words to others. Jesus uses the right words with everyone. Be humble and thoughtful of others. Think before you speak. God want you to have a loving and caring approach when you speak to everyone!

Matthew 12:36-37
Matthew 15:11
Proverbs 15:4

Do Not Let Anyone Intimidate You!

A lot of times, when someone is in a bad mood and the person attack you with insults. They are in an awful mood and they want you to feel miserable also! Try hard to stand still, look at the person and do not say anything, then walk away. That reaction will do more hurt to them, then it will to you. When the intimidator, see that what they are doing is not affecting you. They will feel silly most of the time and walk away. It is very hard for an intimidator to try to bring someone down, when the person show no fear. God want you to show patience, a kind heart with love toward that person. If anything, pray for them. Do not let anyone stop you from receiving your blessing. You stay humble!

Colossians 3:15
Romans 13:10

If You Steal You Will Lie

How do you get to where people see you as not trustworthy? When you do things like lie and steal, people will not trust you! Can you imagine how uncomfortable people would feel, with you being around them, knowing that you steal and is a liar! If you are a person that loves to lie and steal, consider changing your life for the better! Ask the Lord to forgive you for your sins and tell him that you need him to help you. You do not have to steal in order to get what you want. You can work to get it or just ask for it. When you lie about something and you continue to do it. People will think that you are capable of doing anything that is wrong. If you are like this or know someone that have these problems. Pray and ask Jesus to help you and the person with this illness. Jesus will come thru for you. He can save and heal anybody!

Acts 16:30
Jeremiah 5:1
Proverbs 19:1

Eternal Life

Some people hate to think that they could actually have eternal life, when they have had such a hard time here on earth with so many problems. Some are frighten that their life would be the same because they do not understand about eternal life! But all believers can have eternal life. What is so wonderful is that your mortal life when you die, will be changed to eternal life with no more sickness in your body. No more enemies or evil around you. No more sin or ever dying again. You will live forever. If you Love God, believe in Jesus and believe that he died for our sins, and love your neighbors, then there is a chance you will have eternal life. Get into the Bible, study the words. Tell all your friends and enemies about him. Do not miss out on living forever with Jesus and his father in heaven.

Revelation 21:4
Isaiah 25:8
Isaiah 65:19

When you know it is wrong

People every day are doing something that is wrong and could care less. But when you know it is wrong you have to give an account for all your wrong doing. People do wrong so much that when they hear or see it. They try to switch the truth around, to make it the way they want it to be. One main thing that man has changed is to say man can be with a man sexually and a woman can be with a woman sexually. The Bible is God's Holy words and no one is to change his words, ever! Think hard about if you are living in any sin and being disobedient to God's Holy words because one day you are going to have to face Jesus. What would you say?

Leviticus 18:22
Romans 1:18-32
I Corinthians 6:9-11
I Timothy 1:8-10

Never Give Up

There are going to be rugged roads and some heartaches as you go thru life. Never think that you have no one to turn to and help you whenever your heart and mind get burden. It is an awful feeling when problems occur and you feel all alone. So many have given up and gone astray from not getting acquainted with Jesus. They did not know Jesus or tried to get to know the man of God. Do not give up on yourself. Satan wants you to follow him, to fail and destroy yourself and your family. Diligently seek Jesus! Stay close to him! The love that Jesus has for everyone will never go away. Jesus want you to know that if you put your faith in him, serve him and show your love for him, that he will strengthen you and guide you along the way. He is the one that can make things right when so much is going wrong!

Deuteronomy 4:7
Deuteronomy 4: 29-31
II Corinthians 1:24

To Honor: to Respect and Love your Parents is for Life

Although you are getting older and one day you will be living your life on your own, in your own place. No matter where you go in life, always honor your mother and father. This is not saying that you have to obey them, after you have grown up and left home. This is saying that, you should always respect them and show love for them. If your parents try to give you advice on something, never cut them down harshly, as if you think you know it all because you will never know it all! Show some respect and take the time to listen. Honoring them is a good thing and a blessing to you. It respectfully shows your love toward them!

Colossians 3:20
Deuteronomy 5:16

Being Nice is so Easy

What is so bad about being nice? Can you find anything that is so horrible about it? Being nice is good for the immune system! It can also make you feel good about yourself and others. Even when things go bad, it will keep you calm. When you meditate on what God sacred words say: *"The fruit of the spirit is longsuffering, faith, meekness, and temperance."* **Galatians 5:22-23 (KJV).** God's precious words will keep you with a peace of mind, and will help you defeat anything! Be humble, meek and kind to everyone. Pray to God to give you the peace and love to pass on to others!

Colossians 3:13-14
I Corinthians 13:4

Love Suffereth Long

When you are a child of God and you give your life to the Lord. He will step in and help you, to lead you with the Holy Spirit, to direct you on how to love. This should make you so happy! Jesus love never end and he want you to love one another. He wants you not, to have desires to be rude, jealous or have selfishness in your heart. If you take time to look at how kind Jesus is to you, then you can go about doing the same to your fellowman. Jesus do not scream, curse, talk down, or is boastful to you. He shows love, patience, gentleness, humbleness and he take time to listen! He is always ready to help. You do not hear him stump his feet, smack his mouth or suck his teeth. He takes precious time for you. How amazing it is to have a man like Jesus in your life that shows nothing but love and patience. Do the same to others!

I Corinthians 13: 3
Galatians 5:5-6

Get Rid of the Log in your Eye

Do not be so fast to run and complain to others about people you do not like! If Jesus was here today and you hurried up to him, to quickly tell him about someone you do not like. You know what he would tell you!? He would tell you to examine yourself first, then forgive and love the person you are complaining about! Now take time to think about it! When you find fault in someone, and you find it in your heart to just run around and tell everyone you know! Take a look at yourself and check yourself from the inside out! Because you are talking about yourself!

Luke 6:37-38
Luke 6: 41-42

Yes Sir and No Ma'am will take you a long way

Being respectful to people and showing your manners mean a lot. It do not cost you anything to be polite to people; being kind demonstrate that you have a good heart inside of you! Sometimes things will get you down as you go thru life. So many people walk around with hate in their heart, not caring about themselves or anyone else! Some do not know how to show love. They will talk to people any kind of way. You will find as you study the word of God, how to love and forgive. You are to give to people what you want to come back to you and that is love. If you are considerate of other people, stay that way! If you are so full of yourself and think that it is all about you! Pray a sincere prayer to the Lord and ask him to remove that conceitedness from your heart; to forgive you and to fill your heart with love for everyone. Let God show you how to love. Seek to know him. He has an enormous lasting love!

Proverbs 17:22
Psalm 33:13-15

Just Keep on Living

Have you ever heard your friends or family members, sit around and boast about the material things that they have been blessed with? About how they do not get sick like most people and how they have the best children! How they have to shop at certain high class stores and how they have to eat name brand food only! They act as if they have it going on, without even considering ever thanking the Lord for their many blessings. When God bless you with the finer things in life, you are to acknowledge him and thank him for his blessings. Not get the bighead! Praising the Lord for your blessings is something that you should practice to do every day. Though you may not have experience bad times yet! There will come a time when things will get rough along the way. Just keep on living!

Psalm 145:2
Jeremiah 9:23
Galatians 6:14

Have a Goal

It is important to have a goal in life. Believe it or not! There are a great deal of young people, who have never taken the time, to think about what they want out of life. Some teenagers, when they turn eighteen years old, will say in a flash that they are grown! They will go out in the world doing what they want to do, without getting advice from anyone. This is how so many young people waste so much of their time and mess their life up, by stepping out in the world with no plan for their life. Do not be so quick to jump out in the world, not knowing what you want to do in life. Put God in your life and ask him to show you the way. Pray for his love and leadership and let him be your goal!

Philippians 3:14
I Thessalonians 4:11
II Corinthians 5:9
Psalm 73:20

God is Spirit

It is so good to know that you can give God the glory and praise him anytime you get ready. That gives you hope and something to look forward to each day of your life. That mean that when you are at home, at work, on vacation, in your car, at a friend's house, on a bus, at college or on a train, at a restaurant or wherever you are; you can talk to him. Love him, spend time with him and worship him! He is so worthy to be Praise! The Holy Spirit will touch your heart with his love. This love that he gives is for everyone. You are loved!

John 4:24
II Corinthians 3: 17-18

The Mind can be Fooled

Be particular of what you watch on the television and at the movies, this should be taken very seriously. There are so many things that they show on the television and at the movies that can influence you, that many people actually try to copy. You have to remember that you are in a real world, where real things happen, that do not always end with a happy ending. Do not waste your time and mind on watching the television and movies with things that will confuse you about life. God needs to be the center of your life. He can give you the guidance and give you the understanding about life that you need. The Bible is the true picture of life. Let your mind rest on God's Holy words. Not on things that can send you straight to hell!

Proverbs 15:14
Proverbs 11:2

Apply Scripture

When the enemy is surrounded all around you trying to destroy you, which is the evil spirit from Satan that try to attack you from every side. This could be happening at your job, home, church or just about anywhere you go! Search the scriptures and believe and have faith in what God Holy words say about your enemies. The evil spirit can get into anyone. But God will do what he says and fight your battle for you. The scriptures (God's words) are strong and powerful. When you speak his Holy words and rebuke Satan in Jesus name. Satan has to back away from you. He does not like to hear Jesus name or God's Holy words. He will flee away from you! Read the Bible daily. Pray for understanding with a sincere heart and God will bless you with it!

James 4:7-8
Ephesians 6:12

Be Appreciative for being created

At times you may wonder why you were born and why bad things happen to you. In this life there are going to be good and bad days; especially when you are a servant for the Lord. But we are to rejoice in the Lord. Our help for our every need comes from him. Yes, you may get sad but you have something to be joyful about because you were created by him, for something he has special for you to do. We are his marvelous creation! Thank God for creating you!

John 1:3-5
I Corinthians 8:6

The Prayer of the Upright

You know, a sincere prayer do not have to be long. When you know that you have honestly given your life to the Lord, you can find comfort in prayer. You are showing that you love the Lord and that you are trying hard to do what is right. It also shows that you know where to run to, when trouble come. You make it plain to see, that you definitely know where to find relief, and that is in the arms of the Lord. You trust, believe and know that the Lord will answer your prayer. Have you ever felt in your heart, that you were so sure, that whenever you go to someone and ask them for something, that you knew without a doubt that they would give it to you? Well, that is how it is with the Lord. Always have faith without a doubt that when you ask the Lord for something, that he will come thru for you!

Proverbs 15:8
Psalm 125:4
Proverbs 4:18

People Will Talk

Do not fret when people talk bad about you and tell lies about you. As you go thru life serving the Lord. There will always be someone out there that will try to make life hard for you. If you are a very mannerly person and you make good grades on your schoolwork. You are never a problem to your parents and everyone loves you. That is when the enemy will try to attack you. But do not fear! When you let fear comes into your heart. That is when Satan will attack you at your weakest. Do not let that bother you. Be yourself, kind and loving and know that revenge is the Lord's. Do not ever get down to your enemy level. For when you continue to be humble and kind, that is how you run the enemy away. Satan cannot stand kindness or the mention of Jesus name. The more the enemy talks about you and you continue to be humble and respectful. The more the Lord will help you, with many blessings coming your way. Kindness is something else!

Job 20:7-9
Psalm 37: 38-40

God is a Wonderful Provider

Do not sit around and wonder how you are going to make ends meet. Worrying and stress will put you in bad health and kill you! Depend on the Lord and trust him and know that he will provide for you. How I know? His sacred words said that he would. He will provide for you where you will have more than enough for yourself, and you will be able to help someone else in need. God do not lie! His divine words are gospel!

Genesis 22:14
II Corinthians 9:8-10

Jealousy

Do you get jealous of people that look good, dress nice and come from good homes? If you have any jealousy in your heart, you have to want to get rid of it! No one can make you do something that you do not want to do. You can start by asking the Lord to help you, if you really want a changed heart. Are you happy when you hear that a friend, neighbor or family member has been bless with a nice home, clothes, a car, and so many other nice things, or do you get jealous of them? There is no need to get jealous or have a grudge and be envious of them. Becoming jealous will not make you get what they have. You are to be happy with love for them and really mean it from your heart. If you feel as if you cannot shake it off by being jealous of them, pray to the Lord to remove that evil spirit from you and to show you how to love one another. Do not miss your blessings, by dwelling on materialistic things that others have, that are only here temporarily. Set your mind on the Lord that is guaranteed to be with us forever with his love!

Proverbs 14:30
Philippians 2:3-4

Do not wait for something bad to happen to follow Jesus

Why do some people wait for something drastic to happen in their life, before they come to the Lord for help? Is it that they finally realize that no one else can help them? But why something has to go wrong in their life, before they decide to ask for help from Jesus? Do you know that Jesus love you and is always willing to help you, even when people put him on the back burner? This is what it look like, when people make Jesus their last option. When they have tried everything else, and get all sort of crazy suggestions from family and friends. When it looks as if all hope is gone, then they decide to make Jesus their choice. Do not make Jesus your last option! Make him the first one to run to. He has been waiting for the longest to save you!

Luke 15:10
Psalm 103:8
Joel 2: 12-13

Just be Humble

Being humble to the enemy can add so many blessings to your life. As the enemy attack you with harsh words, and bullying, stay humble. This may seem awkward, but the nicer you are to the enemy, they cannot stand it! Learn how to pray for the enemy and wish only good things to come their way and watch how God will bless you. It may sound like a crazy thing to do but it is the right thing to do. Being obedient to God's Holy words is a blessing all by itself. If you love the Lord, then obey him.

I John 4:11
Roman 16:19
II Corinthians 10:6

Greed

Material things are just things. They are going to waste away. Most people want to have it all; gigantic new houses, several new cars, tons of money in the bank -the best of everything. The majority of the time, people seem to forget about God and do not acknowledge him when they are on top. These things cannot bring you happiness. As you accumulate these things, the more you are going to want. Having a relationship with God and being obedient to his words is better than the things of this world. Practice to help others with what God has blessed you with. Think of the needy first as you put yourself last!

Luke 12:15
Luke 12:33
Proverbs 28:22

Racism in School

There is always going to be someone that does not like you. But that is alright because you have a God that loves you. When someone mistreat and seems to have a problem accepting you. Pray for them. There are so many loving people in the world from different race that are so kind and nice to be around. Do not let anyone or anything ruin your day! Satan comes to destroy you and any race of people. He do not care who he hurt. Just be ready for him with your love, meekness and the word of God, with no fear or sadness in your heart. Never think that you have to please someone, to get them to like you. Give all your worries to the Lord! He loves you and will always accept you!

I John 4: 8-10
I John 4: 19-20

You can have so much fun at Bible Study

I never thought that studying the word of God, with a group of people could be so refreshing, so up lifting, so energized; everyone listening, asking question and commenting on the good news about our Lord and Savior Jesus Christ. You learn so much; plus you get to fellowship, hear testimonies of things people have been thru, and how God came thru for them so many times. It is a place where many come to find Jesus, to seek him, to worship and praise him. When you take time to study the word, it makes you want to search further, to learn more about the Lord. It is a feeling like you cannot get enough! Especially if you have a strong desire and love the Lord. The more you study, the more you want to know about him. This is the experience that I have at Bible study. I pray that each person will diligently seek the Lord and tell others about him. Gather your friends and find a good Bible study group. Do not miss out on working for the Lord and doing all that you can do for him! Let this be the day!

Luke 12:31
Hosea 10:12

Seek to be more like Him (Jesus)

As you study the word of God, it will bring you closer to God. You will want to know more and more about the Lord. God did not say that our life would be peaches and cream. No one is perfect in this life but Jesus Christ! *"But we are to have love, joy, peace, kindness, gentleness and self-control."* **- Galatians 5:22 (KJV)**. Pray for the Holy Spirit to live down inside of you! Be a carbon copy and imitate Jesus!

John 13:35
John 15:12
I John 3:14

God will cover you with his Feathers

God is the one that shield you from danger. When you put your faith and trust in the Lord. You do not have to fear, because God has his protection covering you wherever you are. Just to know this, should make you live your life without worrying about anything harming you. Even when you feel as if you are being bullied or mistreated on your job, continue to not worry. You can be content on your job, at school, or wherever you plant your feet. God love you and he watches over you even while you are asleep. His protection with his Holy angels is always right there beside you. So toss fear aside and keep the love that God has for you on your mind!

Psalm 57:1
Psalm 35:2
Psalm 63:6-8

His Words

As you get closer to the Lord, you want his words to soak into you. Almost like being tattooed into your mind. His words tell you all that he can do and will do, if you just trust him! Meditate on his words and trust him! As a young person, sometime you may run into strange things happening to you, that you may not understand. When you are a servant for the Lord, some people will give you a very hard time, when you talk and tell people about the Lord. Teachers, parents and some of your peers will say things that may insult you. But you have to remember what God words say; that you will be persecuted for his sake. This will make you stronger and reassure you, that you are doing something right for the Lord!

Deuteronomy 32:2-3
Matthew 5:11

Be a Mentor

Never be afraid to talk to someone about Jesus. Walk up to the person with love and humbleness. Take some time to talk to your neighbor, a friend, and your peers about Jesus Christ! Tell them that you care about them and that Jesus love them. Tell them how Jesus wants everyone to imitate him in everything that they do! That is something great to know. Giving yourself and time to a person is exactly what Jesus would do. Some people that are lost and do not know about Jesus. Really do not know what to do with themselves when trouble comes. Some will go astray looking for help in drugs, liquor and crime which will lead to destruction. Do not give up on your fellowman. We all need Jesus!

I Thessalonians 2:8
II Timothy 2:2

Create in you a Clean Heart

If you are doing things like going with a married man or woman, talking to your best friend's girlfriend or boyfriend, or you just do not care, who you hurt as long as you get what you want! Stop, pray and ask God to take those desires away from you. Always remember that when you sin you are sinning against God! Everything you do in this world, you will be held liable for on judgment day. Ask God to forgive you of your sins and to have mercy on you. Those sinful desires are not worth missing heaven and be sent straight to hell!

Psalm 51:10
Psalm 78:37

Never take advantage of people

One of the worst things you can do in this life is to try to get over on an elderly person, a handicap person, a poor person, or a widower that is in need for help! Satan is busy every day! Always take time to think before you do or say anything! Times are hard where people will try anything to harm others. Instead of poorly using them, try hard to help them. Ask them do they need help with anything. They may have some chores around their home for you to do. They may need someone to talk to about certain things that might be on their mind. While Jesus was here on earth, He told people how we should love one another. Not just when we run into each other but to always think of others first! To be kind, loving and caring to each other. Remember, when you bless someone, God will bless you!

Proverbs 16:24
Psalm 35:10
Romans 12:13
Psalm 12:5
Hebrews 13:2

Do not ever consider Suicide!

Do you know that God love you no matter what!? Whatever it is that is tearing at you or make you feel as if you are ready to give up and leave this place is evil! Satan comes to steal, to kill and he wants to destroy you! God is waiting for you to come to him, to call on him for help. Please do! You are something that is precious to God. He created you and he only wants the best for you. Everyone have problems. Believe me, no one is perfect but Jesus Christ! When problems come and it gets so bad where you feel as if you cannot bear it or go on. Go to Jesus in prayer and he will hear you and save you. Repent of your sins. Do not let Satan take you away from here! You have a lot to live for and his name is Jesus! He can help you thru anything! Give him a chance! Try him! He will bring you joy, love and peace in your heart. Be that beautiful living testimony and tell the world about Jesus!

Psalms 139: 13-15
Ecclesiastes 11:4-5

Our Mortal Bodies

The good thing to know about after we are raised from the dead is that our bodies will be changed. Our bodies will be superb like Jesus. People that have been thru so much pain in their life or mental impairment will never have to go thru that again. Our bodies will be as spiritual bodies. An eternal body made by God himself. Keep your faith in the Lord. He is eternal, man is temporary!

I Corinthians 15:35-44

Open your Eyes

You do not have to fret when people do you wrong. Never wish anything bad on them. God see and hear everything that goes on in your life! So do not seek revenge or hold a grudge against anyone that hates you. Always have love in your heart for your fellowman. God will protect you from the wicked people. His angels are always around you. Just look around and see that you have nothing to fear. When he protects you, he protects you!

Psalm 91:8
Psalm 31:4
Revelation 3:10

If the Lord had not been on my side

There are many young people that have been targeted and gunned down by plain people and people that work with the police department, that get off with no charges against them. Put your faith and trust in the Lord with no fear in you. When you are approached by someone of high authority with a bad attitude, think about how would Jesus handle it?! He would be very courteous! Be humble, kind, and stand on God's precious words, never doubting that he is on your side and WILL take care of the enemy. Satan wants you to lose your temper! Never go to the level of the person with the attitude. Before you say anything to them, pray a short sincere prayer and ask the Lord to help you and he will. You have to believe that! If you have any doubt in your heart, it will not happen! God is for real! Use the love that you have in your heart for everyone and LIVE!

Psalm 124:1, 7-8
Psalm 115:15

The Thoughts of the Wicked

Always think before you speak, especially if you are angry at someone. If you take time to catch a deep breath and calm down before you speak, it will make you a healthier person. Harsh words can cause so much damage to someone, plus it will raise your blood pressure. A wicked person does not care about who they hurt. They talk to people with evil and hate in their heart. They carry a grudge around for anyone they run into. They are unhappy and they are out and about trying to make any and every one unhappy. They are miserable and they do not stop with their bad behavior until they make someone else miserable. Carefully plan your words before you speak!

Proverbs 15:28
Proverbs 10:19, 32
Amos: 5: 13

Do not Blame Others

When you have made an honest mistake, always tell the truth about what really happen. Sometimes when you are young, you may think that it is okay to overlook, when you do something wrong and not tell anyone. Others could suffer if you do not speak up and explain what really occurred. A lot of times, when things go wrong in life, people love to try to put the blame on someone else. Do not be afraid to own up to what you did, that turned out wrong. God will always be there for you, even in times of trouble. Do not run from him. Go to him with all of your wrong doings and confess to him what you have done. It will make you feel so much better and you will love yourself a lot better!

Hosea 4:4
Amos 5:14

Upright and Devoted to God

Although you are around sinful people every day of your life, do not get weak in your faith. God want you to live a lifestyle that is healthy and loving. Do not let what other people do, that is wrong, change you. Your friends might say, oh it is okay to have one drink of liquor, or take one drag of marijuana or sniff cocaine, it will not hurt you. They may say, it is okay to tell one lie, or steal this for me, no one will ever know. God will know! Learn how to stand strong on doing what is right and never be so easy to let anyone persuade you into doing wrong. Let the word of God sink into your heart and mind and be happy about it! Remember, you do not have to prove anything to your friends or anybody. Stay close to the Lord, imitate him and think about what he would do!

Proverbs 3:33
Proverbs 15:15

You should be ashamed to Bully

When certain students at school come to school, dressed different without name brand clothes on, be respectful to them. Everyone is made different, think different and look different. Many families cannot afford name brand clothes to dress their children in. Which is really something that most parents do not seem to think is important and they are right! Education is the main base for school and that is what students need to focus on. Not what you wear, or who's popular and who's not, or who is so smart! This is where the jealousy and hate with envy get started. The word of God says that we are to love everyone, no matter what race or color! Bullying comes from people that are jealous, of something that they see a person has, that they want. It could be the person has a great personality, good looks, the way they talk, walk or whatever uniqueness that they have, the bully envies it! So they zero in on the person with a horrible evil, to make them afraid to succeed with their uniqueness by bullying them. They try hard to break the intelligent person down! One way to handle this is to treat the bully with kindness, and to never show fear. If you show fear, it will keep the bully in your ever presence to attack you! When you show kindness to the bully, God will not let any harm come to you. The hole that the bullies dig for you, they will be the one that fall in it!

I Peter 3:8-9
Matthew 5:43-45
Romans 12:19-21

Deuteronomy 31:6
Psalm 18:3
Isaiah 41:11-13
Psalm 121:2

Stop trying to keep up with the Jones

Be who you are and do not worry about what shoes, clothes, car or house or how much money other people are blessed with. It is a sad thing to try to do what you see other people do and try to get things that you know you cannot afford, just to try to keep up with them. You should not dwell on what other people are doing. Have a mind to do what you like in life! If you envy or have jealousy in your heart toward people, do some serious praying to the Lord and tell him that you need him to help you! What is so hard about being happy for people that have nice things? When you have a jealous streak in your heart, it really shows that you do not know what you want in life! Because if you did, you would not be so worried about what the other person have or is doing! Ask God to strengthen you, to have a mind of your own and to direct your path! To let it be about him and not about money and material things of this world!

Luke 12:15
Ecclesiastes: 5:13-15

Take your complaints to God

If you have problems at home, at school, on the job, at church, or anywhere! Talk to the Lord about it first. Tell him about your situation. He already knows about it. But you have to go to him with faith and trust in him and believe that he can help you! There is no need to complain to anyone else about your problems because they cannot make it right. God can take your complaints. He hears when you cry for help! Do not ever try to handle the problem on your own. You have God, who has a son name Jesus Christ! He has never lost a case. Change your way of living. Love him and diligently seek him. He is waiting to hear from you!

Psalm 39:1-3
Psalm 141:3

God's Holy Words will protect you

As you study God's holy words, try to memorize them. The scriptures are powerful words from God that can save you. Memorizing the scriptures is something that no one can take away from you. There will come a day, when there will be evil people, trying to destroy every Bible out there. So memorize God's Holy words. When you speak God's Holy words to the enemy, they have to leave your surroundings. When you are obedient to God's Holy words, you will see how his powerful words will come thru for you. The Bible has a concordance that is located at the back of the Bible. Do not hesitate to read them. God has the answer for your problems. God words are the truth and they show you how to live and love him and how to love others!

Psalm 5:11
Psalm 31:2

361

Prayer is the Answer

What do you do when trouble is all around you? The neighbor had your dog put to sleep because it killed their cat! You lose your purse or wallet with all of your money in it! You get a failing grade on an essay that you worked really hard on. Your family gets an eviction notice! Your mother and father split up! You start getting bullied at school! There are so many bad things going on in your life where you are ready to just give up! Things like this happen to people every day. But when you do not know how to deal with these problems Satan will step in to really destroy you! I have to tell you about someone name Jesus. A lot of people act very uncomfortable when you talk to them about Jesus. But he is the one to get real with because he is the one that will help you and never throw it back in your face. Pray to him about all of your problems. Pray and ask him to forgive you of your sins and to show you the way. He will show you that he is the WAY!

Colossians 4:2
Luke 18:6-8

Show Your Love

Turn from your evil ways. Have faith in God. In all that you do, always put God first! God should be your first priority. When you wake up in the morning, praise and thank him for watching over you, all thru the night and ask him to watch over you all thru the day. Just knowing that you have God first in your life, should keep you with a peace of mind and a smile on your face. Tell all of your friends about him and pray that they will change their lives to live for him. Get busy and be a servant for the Lord and show your love for him!

Psalm 100:2,5
Psalm 40: 10-11

Faith it

I love a parent or guardian that encourages their children. Encouraging words are something that really make you want to push forward and not give up. When a parent or guardian tell you that, even though you may have failed doing something, but they know that you will do better the next time. Trust their word, because it shows that they have faith in you and that they love you. Put faith in God and ask him to help you along the way. Faith is an example that is used every day. By showing it, not talking it! Walk by faith; be obedient of faith, by keeping the faith!

II Timothy 1:5
Hebrews 6:11-12

My Heart Belong to you

Love the Lord with all of your heart. Ask him; what can you do for him? He has shown us over and over again how much he loves us all. You know when you search the Bible and learn about him. You will see that he taught about love and how to spread and share it, while he was here on earth. He taught about peace and poor people in need and how to love one another, how to always be caring toward the widowers, and how to freely give and to think of others and to put them first! He is all about love. Not about being mean and hateful to people! Give your very best to him and praise and thank him each and every day of your life. Give your heart body and soul to him. Be a servant for the Lord and do it from your heart!

Colossians 3:2
Matthew 22:37
Psalm 27:8
Psalm 57:7
I Kings 8:61

Delight yourself in Jesus

When you diligently seek the Lord, praise him as you work and be a servant for him! Know that God will always fight your battle for you. To be able to delight in Jesus, you have to get to know him. Start a close relationship with him in prayer, in Bible study and quiet time! Talk to him, love him and praise and thank him for everything he has ever done for you. As you draw close to him. Commit yourself by trusting him with your life, and your family and believe that he will take care of your every need.

Psalm 37:4
Jeremiah 15:16

Healthy Self-Esteem

Having the Lord on your side is such a beautiful blessing. He can keep you strong with a firm mind, to never doubt yourself, if you obey his Holy words. If you try it, he will quickly show you how you are valuable to him. He created you in his own image. Anything in his image is nothing but good. So do not say bad discouraging things about yourself or others. We are all beautiful in his sight! He is our father. Always think and feel good about yourself. He loves everything about you because he created you and he did not just create you. He created you for a reason, a purpose to be here in this world. Pray, talk to him and ask him, what is your purpose?! When you are feeling down and very sad, encourage yourself and thank God for creating you. Know and believe that you will always be very valuable to him!

Romans 12:3
Psalm 139:13-16

Faith Miracles

If you can put your trust in the Lord and have faith the size of a mustard seed, there will be nothing impossible for the Lord, when it comes to helping you. A mustard seed is very, very tiny. God do not ask you for a lot. He wants you to know him and to come to him with all of your worries. God will come thru for you, when everyone else has said no to you so many times. You could have been turned down for a job. You did not make it on a sports team or as a cheer leader. People rejected you as a friend with so many no's and doubt everywhere you turn. Faith can be strong, if you have faith in God without a doubt! Keep your heart and mind on Jesus. Concentrate on him and not things that try to take your mind off of Jesus. Focus with all of your heart, that the Lord will come thru for you. Stay strong forever on your faith in him. Truly he is the miracle worker!

Hebrews 12:1-4
Hebrews 10:32-34

The Sun Shine on the Just and Unjust

If you pay attention to life, you will see that good things happen to the good and bad people. Do not go around wondering why good things always happen to bad people! When me and my friends were in high school, we would always see some kids that would never have any respect for their elders. They would curse a lot around them and steal and tell a lie in a minute. They were the ones that would always end up with the nice guys or girl that came from nice homes. Me and my friends could not figure it out! We were saying; I am a good person, and nothing but bad things come our way. It always seemed as if all the good guys were taken by the bad girls! But that was not the case. We were too busy watching what they were doing, instead of noticing how God was blessing us also. When you are living right for the Lord and loving him. Satan will attack and try to block anything good from happening to you. Just keep the love in your heart for your fellowman with a peace of mind. Remember that God see everything and truly he has something good up the road for you also! Just keep loving him and everyone and keep your faith!

Leviticus 19:18
Matthew 5:45

My Help Comes From the Lord

You are always going to need the Lord. You know why? Because you cannot make it in this world without him. He is the one that keep you safe with the covering of his angels. He watches over you 24-7 and his love for you is everlasting. He reassures you every day from his love and protection that he is on your side! This should keep you with joy and happiness in your heart, just to know that he love you and will never leaves you. So no matter what problems may occur at school, home, or wherever you may be in this world, always trust in the Lord knowing that he will always come thru for you. He will always do what he promised you!

Psalm 121
Revelation 7:16

Do Unto Others

If you love God, loving others should come natural to you. You are to always have kindness, love and respect for everyone. Even people that do not like or care for you! You will notice as you mature in life, that you will meet all kind of people. Some with good and bad personalities that might care only for themselves, but do not let that throw you off track. Lean on God's powerful words! Be truthful and honest to people. Judge no one! Greet people with a smile. Show love toward your fellowman. This is a lifesaving and healthy way to live. God's way is the best way, if you truly love the Lord!

Matthew 7:12
I John 4:20
Galatians 5:14

Your Sins Will Find You Out!

You can fool man but you will never be able to fool or trick God! A lot of people think that because they do not see God, there is no God. But there is a mighty God that sees everything you do and hear every word that comes out of your mouth. He even knows what you are thinking! You are fooling yourself when you go out in the world doing sinful things and think that just because you were not caught, that you got away with it! God saw it and he know all about it! Turn from your evil and sinful ways and sincerely ask the Lord to help you! He loves you even though you are sinning and living a sinful life. He wants to help you. But you have to make your mind up to either live for him or Satan! To live for him is to gain! To live for Satan is to lose! Repent of your sins; ask for forgiveness while you can. Tomorrow is not promised to you!

Numbers 32:23
James 5:16
Acts 3:19

Omnipresent

It is a beautiful thing to know that no matter where you are in this world. God will always be present with you! Just to know that God is with you everywhere, should keep your mind in splendor serenity. Each day, get closer to him in his words and enjoy his present. He is on the bus, on the train, on the plane, at the park, at your school, in your class or wherever you rest your feet. God is not going anywhere! Magnify him and be thankful for him. Give him the praise each and every day of your life and rejoice because he loves you!

Psalm 139:7-12
Jeremiah 23:24

Do not Skip Church

So many people do not want to go near a church, when they are feeling down with so many burdens hanging heavy on their mind. Some feel as if going to church will not help their circumstances. Do not ever let your friends, your problems and your trials and tribulations stop you from going to church. The church is where there are so many blessings for you. God is there and he is waiting for any and every one that comes to him for help. There you can find love, encouragement, healing, strength, and the Lord. Instead of bypassing the church, take a running start to always be the first one there to receive your blessings and be blessed!

Hebrews 10:25
Hebrews 3:13

Advocate-I John 2:1
Anchor-Hebrews 6:19
Almighty-Rev. 1:8
Alpha and Omega-Rev. 22:13
Apostle-Hebrews 3:1
Beginning-Col. 1:18
Bishop of your Souls-I Peter 2:25
Blessed and only Ruler-I Tim. 6:15
Bread of Life-John 6:48
Bright and Morning Star-Rev. 22:16
Carpenter's Son-Matt. 13:55
Chief Shepherd-I Peter 5:4
Comforter-Isaiah-61:2
Counselor-Isaiah-9:6
Creator-Colossians 1:16
Deliverer-Romans 11:26
Door-John 10:7,9
Everlasting Father-Isaiah 9:6
Faithful Witness-Rev. 1:5
First and Last-Rev. 1:17
Firstborn-Matt 1:25
Foundation-Isaiah 28:16
Fountain-Jer. 2:13
Governor-Matt. 2:6
Great High Priest-Hebrews 4:14
Head-Eph. 4:15
Helper-Hebrews 13:6
Holy and Righteous One-Acts 3:14
Horn of Salvation-Luke 1:69
I Am-John 8:58
Immanuel-Isaiah 7:14
Jehovah-Isaiah 26:4
King Eternal Immortal Invisible-I Tim. 1:17

King of Kings-I Tim. 6:15
King of the Jews-Matt. 2:2
Lamb-Rev. 13:8
Lawgiver-Isaiah 33:22
Life-John 14:6
Light of the World-John 8:12
Master-Matt. 8:19
Mediator-I Tim. 2:5
Messenger of the Covenant-Malachi 3:1
Messiah-Daniel 9:25
Nazarene-Matt. 2:23
Prince of Peace-Isaiah 9:6
Prophet-Luke 24:19
Redeemer-Job 19:25
Resurrection and Life-John 11:25
Righteous One-Acts 7:52
Rock-I Cor. 10:4
Rose of Sharon-Song of Solomon 2:1
Savior-Luke 2:11
Seed of Abraham-Gal. 3:16
Shepherd and Overseer-I Peter 2:25
Son of David-Matt. 1:1
Son of Man-Matt. 8:20
Son of the most High-Luke 1:32
True Light-John 1:9
True Vine-John 15:1
Truth-John 14:6
Way-John 14:6
Witness-Isaiah 55:4
Wonderful-Isaiah 9:6
Word-John 1:1
YAHWEH-Isaiah 26:4

Always keep God first in your life!

About the Author

Maryjane Edwards is on a mission for the Lord. She has an everlasting love for God and people. Having the experience of working with inmates and juveniles as a Correctional Officer directed her to reach out to spread the gospel about our Lord and savior, Jesus Christ. She has a passion about her to touch the young and anyone that do not know the Lord. She is a speaker at a local nursing facility for the elderly which teaches them about the word of God, which she has been doing for four years. She also teaches adult Sunday school class twice a month at her church. She has an Associate degree in Paralegal and she is a licensed Cosmetologist. She is a gospel playwright with a God given talent to write "Come By Here Lord" a play that the Holy Spirit placed in her heart. She is the author of a children's fairy tale, "Dontayan" and the book, "Jesus the Anchor". She has completed her third year in Biblical and Theological Studies. Her goal is to be a servant for the Lord and to spread the good news about Jesus Christ. Young people all over the world and people that do not know the Lord are struggling thru life. This book will touch the heart of anyone that dares to read it. I encourage you today to read this book. It will send you in the right direction and that is to God. He will change your whole life! Truly he is worthy to be praised!

Made in the USA
Columbia, SC
24 June 2021

40290245R00222